GREEK MYTHOLOGY
A COLLECTION OF CAPTIVATING GREEK MYTHS

JORDAN LONG

CONTENTS

INTRODUCTION

Greek mythology has captivated the minds and imaginations of people for millennia, weaving together tales of gods, heroes, monsters, and epic adventures that have shaped the cultural landscape of the Western world. From the thunderous wrath of Zeus to the tragic fate of Oedipus, these stories offer a window into the beliefs, values, and imagination of the ancient Greeks. They are not merely tales of the past; they are narratives that continue to resonate, inspire, and teach us about the complexities of human nature and the mysteries of the universe.

This book, Greek Mythology: A Collection of Captivating Greek Myths, aims to serve as a comprehensive guide to the rich and diverse world of Greek mythology. It is designed to be accessible to both beginners who are new to the mythology and seasoned readers who wish to deepen their understanding of these timeless stories. Whether you are seeking to explore the intricate relationships between the gods or to immerse yourself in the heroic quests and tragic tales of ancient Greece, this collection provides a well-rounded and engaging exploration of one of the most influential mythological traditions in human history.

The journey begins with an introduction to the Pantheon of Greek Gods & Goddesses, offering insights into the divine figures who rule over the heavens, earth, and underworld. Understanding these deities is essential, as they play pivotal roles in the myths that follow. The second chapter shifts focus to the heroes, demi-gods, and legendary figures—those extraordinary characters whose feats of bravery, cunning, and endurance have earned them a place in the annals of Greek mythology. In the third chapter, we delve into the world of monsters and mythical creatures, exploring the fearsome beings that challenge the gods and heroes alike.

The fourth chapter offers a glimpse into the daily life of the ancient Greeks and examines how they worshipped their gods. Understanding the context in which these myths were created provides valuable insights into the cultural and religious practices of the time.

Following these foundational chapters, the book transitions into the heart of Greek mythology: the myths themselves. From the dawn of creation to the fall of Troy, each chapter recounts one of the major myths that have captivated audiences for centuries. These stories are not just about the gods and heroes; they are about the eternal struggles between order and chaos, love and loss, fate and free will.

The myths covered in this book span a wide range of legendary tales, beginning with the Greek Creation Myth and continuing through stories such as The Titanomachy, The 12 Labors of Heracles, The Trojan War, and The Odyssey. Each myth is presented in detail, offering readers an immersive experience into the world of ancient Greece.

Whether you are reading these myths for the first time or revisiting them with fresh eyes, Greek Mythology: A Collection of Captivating Greek Myths invites you to embark on a journey through the timeless stories that have shaped human thought and culture. As you turn the pages, you will encounter the grandeur, the tragedy, and the enduring power of Greek mythology—a tradition that continues to captivate and inspire, reminding us of the universal themes that bind us across time and space.

CHAPTER 1: THE PANTHEON OF GREEK GODS & GODDESSES

There are many different Greek Gods and Goddesses, categorized into three primary groups: the primordial deities, the Titans, and the Olympians. The primordial deities represent the first wave, embodying the fundamental elements of the universe. The Titans, the second wave, are the offspring of the primordial deities and represent more specific aspects of the natural world. Finally, the Olympians, who are the focus of most Greek myths, represent the third wave and are the descendants of the Titans.

In this chapter, we will introduce you to each of these deities, providing a brief overview of their backgrounds, lineages, and roles in Greek mythology. This chapter is designed to be flexible; you can choose to read it in its entirety to familiarize yourself with the pantheon, or you can refer to it as you encounter these deities in the myths throughout the book.

For ease of reference, the deities within each section are listed in alphabetical order. This structure ensures that you can quickly find the information you need, whether you're reading about the primordial forces that shaped the cosmos, the Titans who ruled before the Olympians, or the well-known gods and goddesses of Mount Olympus.

The Primordial Deities

The Primordial Deities are the first beings to emerge at the dawn of creation, representing the fundamental elements and forces of the universe. These ancient gods embody concepts such as the earth, sky, sea, and love, forming the very fabric of existence. Their influence is pervasive, setting the stage for the birth of the Titans and the Olympian gods, and their roles in Greek mythology are foundational, shaping the cosmos and the lives of the gods and mortals that follow.

Aether

Aether is the primordial deity representing the pure, upper air that the gods breathe, as opposed to the normal air mortals inhale. He is the personification of the bright, glowing upper sky and is often associated with the daylit sky. Aether is the offspring of Erebus (Darkness) and Nyx (Night), and the brother of Hemera (Day). Aether's role in Greek mythology, though not as prominent as other deities, is crucial as he embodies the essence of brightness and light, signifying the clear and pure air that the gods dwell in, distinct from the earthly realm of humans.

Ananke

Ananke is the primordial goddess personifying necessity, inevitability, and fate. Often depicted with her consort, Chronos (Time), she is seen as a serpentine figure entwined with him, encircling the primal world egg and constraining the universe's creation. Ananke is considered one of the most powerful deities, as she represents the unalterable forces that dictate the cosmos and the lives of gods and mortals alike. Her influence underscores the inescapable nature of destiny and the natural order, making her a fundamental force in the mythological framework of Greek cosmology.

Chaos

Chaos is the primordial void from which all existence sprang. Often described as a vast, dark, and formless abyss, Chaos is the first entity to emerge at the dawn of creation. From Chaos, the primordial deities Gaia (Earth), Tartarus (the Abyss), Eros (Love), Erebus (Darkness), and Nyx (Night) were born. Chaos represents the initial state of the universe, embodying the concept of disorder and potential, from which the ordered cosmos and all life eventually arose. As such, Chaos plays a foundational role in Greek mythology, symbolizing the origin of everything and the underlying fabric of reality.

Chronos

Chronos is the primordial god personifying time itself, often depicted as an incorporeal force governing the endless progression of existence. Not to be confused with the Titan Cronus, Chronos represents the abstract, inexorable flow of time that shapes the universe. Often seen alongside his consort Ananke (Necessity), he is described as a serpentine figure entwined with her, encircling the primordial world egg. Chronos's role is fundamental, as he embodies the relentless and eternal passage of time, influencing the creation, growth, and decay of all things in the cosmos.

Erebus

Erebus is the primordial deity and personification of deep darkness and shadow. Born from Chaos, Erebus is one of the earliest beings to emerge at the dawn of creation. He is often associated with the underworld and the region through which souls must pass to reach Hades. Erebus is the consort of Nyx (Night), and together they parented several deities, including Aether (Brightness) and Hemera (Day). Erebus's role in mythology underscores the duality of light and dark, and he represents the obscurity and depth of the shadowy realms, providing a necessary balance to the brightness of existence.

Eros

Eros is the primordial god of love and desire, often depicted as a powerful force driving the creation and attraction in the universe. According to some myths, Eros emerged from Chaos, while other traditions describe him as the son of Aphrodite and Ares. As a primordial deity, Eros's influence extends beyond romantic love, embodying the fundamental creative force that brings harmony and unity to the cosmos. His role is essential in the mythology, as he incites passion and bonds between gods and mortals, ensuring the continuity and dynamism of life. Eros's presence highlights the intrinsic power of love and desire in shaping both the divine and mortal realms.

Gaia (Gaea)

Gaia is the primordial goddess and personification of the Earth, often revered as the great mother of all life. Born from Chaos, Gaia emerged as one of the first beings in the universe, embodying the fertile ground from which all existence sprang. She is the mother of numerous deities and creatures, including Uranus (the Sky), the Titans, the Giants, and the Cyclopes. Gaia's role is fundamental, as she provides the foundation for life and supports the natural world. Her influence extends to various myths and legends, where she is often involved in the creation and sustenance of the cosmos, highlighting her vital importance in Greek mythology.

Hemera

Hemera is the primordial goddess of day and daylight. She is the daughter of Erebus (Darkness) and Nyx (Night), making her part of the initial generation of deities that emerged from Chaos. Hemera personifies the bright and radiant light of day, driving away the shadows of night each morning. Her role is to bring light and clarity to the world, creating the cycle of day and night. Hemera's daily emergence from the Underworld as her mother Nyx descends symbolizes the ever-repeating cycle of time and the balance between darkness and light in the natural world.

Hypnos

Hypnos is the primordial god of sleep, providing rest and tranquility to both gods and mortals. He is the son of Nyx (Night) and Erebus (Darkness), and the twin brother of Thanatos (Death), residing in the realm of eternal night. Hypnos is often depicted as a gentle and calming figure, sometimes portrayed with wings on his temples, symbolizing the swift and peaceful nature of sleep. His role is essential in mythology, as he ensures the restorative power of sleep, allowing beings to rejuvenate and find peace. Hypnos's influence underscores the importance of rest and the natural cycles of life and death.

Nyx

Nyx is the primordial goddess of the night, embodying the power and mystery of darkness. Born from Chaos, she is one of the earliest deities in the Greek pantheon. Nyx is the mother of many significant deities, including Hypnos (Sleep), Thanatos (Death), Erebus (Darkness), Hemera (Day), and Aether (Brightness), often through parthenogenesis or with Erebus as her consort. She resides in the shadows of the Underworld, emerging each evening to blanket the world in night. Nyx's role is fundamental, as she represents the duality of existence, balancing light and dark, and is often depicted as a powerful and enigmatic figure whose influence commands respect from both gods and mortals.

Phanes

Phanes is a primordial deity representing the force of creation and the emergence of life. Often depicted as a radiant, winged figure, Phanes is associated with the Orphic cosmogony and is considered the firstborn of the gods, emerging from the cosmic egg laid by Chronos (Time) and Ananke (Necessity). As the personification of procreation and the bringer of light, Phanes is credited with creating the universe and all its beings. His role is to illuminate the cosmos and initiate the cycle of life, making him a fundamental force in the Orphic tradition, symbolizing the power of creation, light, and the birth of existence.

Pontus

Pontus is the primordial god of the sea, representing the vast, untamed waters of the world. He is one of the earliest deities, born from Gaia (Earth) without a consort. Pontus personifies the deep sea and all marine life, embodying the mysterious and powerful nature of the ocean. He is the father of several sea deities and creatures, including Nereus, Thaumas, Phorcys, Ceto, and Eurybia, through his union with Gaia. Pontus's role in mythology is fundamental, as he symbolizes the ancient and boundless waters that are integral to the creation and sustenance of life on Earth.

Tartarus

Tartarus is both a primordial deity and a vast, dark abyss used as a dungeon of torment and suffering for the wicked. Born from Chaos, Tartarus is one of the earliest entities to emerge in the Greek cosmological order. As a place, Tartarus lies deep beneath the Earth, even below Hades, and serves as a prison for the Titans after their defeat by the Olympian gods. It is also the dwelling place of other monstrous beings and souls condemned for their sins. Tartarus's role is crucial in maintaining the cosmic balance, representing the ultimate punishment and the darkest depths of the world, contrasting with the divine realms of the gods.

Thalassa

Thalassa is the primordial goddess and personification of the sea. She is one of the early deities born from Aether (Brightness) and Hemera (Day). Thalassa represents the Mediterranean Sea and all the waters that nourish and sustain life on Earth. Often depicted as a serene and nurturing figure, she is the mother of various sea creatures and entities, including the Telchines and the sea nymphs. Thalassa's role in mythology underscores the importance of the sea as a source of life, fertility, and sustenance, highlighting her vital influence on both the natural world and the mythological cosmos.

Uranus

Uranus is the primordial god personifying the sky and the heavens. He emerged from Chaos and, together with Gaia (Earth), formed one of the earliest divine couples. Uranus and Gaia's union produced the Titans, the Cyclopes, and the Hecatoncheires (Hundred-Handed Giants). Uranus's role in mythology is significant as he represents the sky's overarching dome and its union with the Earth, symbolizing the structure and order of the cosmos. However, his reign was marked by tyranny, as he imprisoned his monstrous offspring deep within Gaia, leading to his eventual overthrow by his son Cronus, who castrated him at Gaia's urging. Uranus's fall from power set the stage for the rise of the Titans and the subsequent rule of the Olympian gods.

First Generation Titans

The First Generation of Titans are the children of the primordial deities, ruling during the Golden Age of Greek mythology. These powerful beings represent various aspects of the natural world and human experience, such as time, intellect, and memory. Led by Cronus, they held dominion over the cosmos until they were overthrown by their own offspring, the Olympians, in the epic battle known as the Titanomachy. The Titans' legacy endures through both their direct descendants and the myths that explore themes of power, rebellion, and transformation.

Coeus

Coeus is one of the Titans, the offspring of Uranus (Sky) and Gaia (Earth). Known as the Titan of intelligence and the axis of heaven, Coeus represents the inquisitive mind and the quest for knowledge. He married his sister Phoebe, the Titaness of prophecy and intellect, and together they had two daughters: Leto, the mother of Apollo and Artemis, and Asteria, the goddess of falling stars. Coeus played a significant role in the early divine hierarchy, but like the other Titans, he was overthrown by the Olympian gods during the Titanomachy and imprisoned in Tartarus. His legacy, through his descendants, continued to influence the Olympian order and the domain of knowledge and prophecy.

Crius

Crius is one of the Titans, the offspring of Uranus (Sky) and Gaia (Earth). He is often associated with the constellations and the measure of the year, embodying aspects of time and the celestial axis. Crius married his sister Eurybia, a daughter of Gaia and Pontus, and they had three children: Astraeus, Pallas, and Perses. These offspring further linked Crius to the stars, war, and destruction. Like the other Titans, Crius played a crucial role in the early cosmic order but was eventually overthrown by the Olympian gods during the Titanomachy and imprisoned in Tartarus. His legacy continued through his children, who influenced various domains in Greek mythology, particularly those related to the heavens and time.

Cronus

Cronus is the youngest of the Titans and the son of Uranus (Sky) and Gaia (Earth). Known as the god of time and the harvest, Cronus is often depicted with a sickle, the tool he used to overthrow his tyrannical father Uranus. After castrating Uranus, Cronus became the ruler of the cosmos during the Golden Age, a period of peace and prosperity. He married his sister Rhea, and together they had several children, including the Olympian gods Zeus, Hera, Poseidon, Hades, Demeter, and Hestia. However, fearing a prophecy that he would be overthrown by one of his offspring, Cronus swallowed each of his children at birth. This cycle of fear and power was broken when Rhea hid their youngest child, Zeus, who eventually grew up to challenge and defeat Cronus, leading to the rise of the Olympian gods and the end of the Titan's dominion.

Hyperion

Hyperion is one of the twelve Titans, the children of Uranus (Sky) and Gaia (Earth). He is often associated with light and the heavenly bodies, earning the title "The High One" or "He Who Goes Above." Hyperion married his sister Theia, the Titaness of sight and the shining light of the clear blue sky, and together they had three significant offspring: Helios (the Sun), Selene (the Moon), and Eos (the Dawn). Hyperion's role in mythology underscores the importance of light and celestial phenomena. As the father of these essential deities, he represents the natural cycles of day and night, as well as the passage of time marked by the movements of the sun, moon, and dawn. Hyperion's legacy continues through his children, who play vital roles in maintaining the balance and order of the cosmos.

Iapetus

Iapetus is one of the twelve Titans, the offspring of Uranus (Sky) and Gaia (Earth). Often associated with mortality and craftsmanship, Iapetus is sometimes referred to as the "Piercer," indicative of his role in the cosmos. He married the Oceanid Clymene, and together they had several notable children, including Atlas, Prometheus, Epimetheus, and Menoetius. Each of his offspring played significant roles in various myths, particularly in the interactions between gods and mortals. Iapetus's role in mythology is crucial as he represents the generational link between the primordial deities and the later gods and humans. His legacy is especially significant through Prometheus, who defied the gods by giving fire to humanity, symbolizing the enduring struggle and interplay between divine authority and human ingenuity.

Mnemosyne

Mnemosyne is the Titaness of memory and remembrance, and the mother of the Nine Muses. She is the daughter of Uranus (Sky) and Gaia (Earth), and her name means "memory" in Greek. Mnemosyne's union with Zeus, the king of the gods, resulted in the birth of the Muses, who preside over the arts and sciences and inspire creativity and knowledge in humanity. Mnemosyne's role is fundamental in the realm of myth and culture, as memory is crucial for the preservation and transmission of knowledge, history, and traditions. Through her daughters, Mnemosyne's influence extends to all forms of artistic and intellectual expression, making her an essential figure in the pantheon of Greek mythology.

Oceanus

Oceanus is one of the twelve Titans, the offspring of Uranus (Sky) and Gaia (Earth). He is the personification of the vast, encircling river that was believed to flow around the world, encompassing all the Earth's waters. Oceanus is often depicted as a serene, bearded figure with a crab-claw crown and fish-like features. He married his sister Tethys, and together they produced the Oceanids, a multitude of river gods and sea nymphs who inhabited every freshwater body on Earth. Oceanus's role in mythology is significant as he represents the boundless, all-encompassing nature of the world's waters, serving as the source of all rivers, seas, and lakes, and highlighting the essential role of water in the natural world.

Phoebe

Phoebe is one of the twelve Titans, the children of Uranus (Sky) and Gaia (Earth). She is associated with the prophetic powers of the Oracle of Delphi and is often linked to the moon and its luminous qualities. Phoebe married her brother Coeus, and together they had two daughters, Leto and Asteria. Through Leto, she is the grandmother of the Olympian twins Apollo and Artemis. Phoebe's role in mythology highlights her as a figure of intellect and prophecy, and she is sometimes referred to as the "bright" or "radiant" Titaness, emphasizing her connection to light and wisdom. Her legacy is carried on through her descendants, particularly in the domains of prophecy, the moon, and the celestial realms.

Rhea

Rhea is one of the twelve Titans and the daughter of Uranus (Sky) and Gaia (Earth). Known as the "Great Mother," she is the goddess of fertility, motherhood, and generation. Rhea is married to her brother Cronus, and together they are the parents of the first generation of Olympian gods: Zeus, Hera, Poseidon, Hades, Demeter, and Hestia. Her role in mythology is crucial, as she is pivotal in the transition of power from the Titans to the Olympians. To save her children from being swallowed by Cronus, who feared a prophecy that he would be overthrown by one of his offspring, Rhea hid her youngest son, Zeus, and tricked Cronus by giving him a stone wrapped in swaddling clothes to swallow instead. Zeus eventually grew up to fulfill the prophecy, leading to the Olympians' rise to power and the fall of the Titans. Rhea's actions underscore her importance as a protector of her children and a key figure in the continuation of divine lineage.

Tethys

Tethys is one of the twelve Titans and the daughter of Uranus (Sky) and Gaia (Earth). She is the Titaness of the nourishing flow of fresh water and is often associated with the fertile aspects of the natural world. Tethys married her brother Oceanus, the Titan of the vast, encircling river that was believed to flow around the world. Together, they produced the Oceanids, a multitude of water nymphs, and the river gods who preside over all the freshwater bodies on Earth. Tethys's role in mythology is significant as she represents the life-giving and nurturing aspects of water, essential for sustaining both the natural world and human life. Her offspring are essential figures in various myths, highlighting the importance of rivers and springs in Greek cosmology.

Theia

Theia is one of the twelve Titans and the daughter of Uranus (Sky) and Gaia (Earth). Known as the Titaness of sight and the shining light of the clear blue sky, Theia embodies the divine light that makes vision possible and illuminates the world. She married her brother Hyperion, the Titan of light, and together they had three significant offspring: Helios (the Sun), Selene (the Moon), and Eos (the Dawn). Theia's role in mythology is crucial as she represents the source of all light and brightness, essential for life and growth. Her children, who personify the major celestial bodies, further emphasize her influence over the natural cycles of day and night and the passage of time.

Themis

Themis is one of the twelve Titans and the daughter of Uranus (Sky) and Gaia (Earth). She is the personification of divine law, order, and justice, often depicted holding scales or a cornucopia. Themis played a crucial role as a counselor to Zeus, the king of the gods, and was revered for her wisdom and fairness. She is the mother of the Horae (the goddesses of the natural order and the seasons) and the Moirai (the Fates), emphasizing her influence over the fundamental principles that govern both the cosmos and human society. Themis's role underscores the importance of justice and balance, ensuring harmony within the divine and mortal realms.

Second Generation Titans

The Second Generation of Titans includes the offspring of the original Titans who did not become Olympians. These gods often embody more specific natural phenomena and human qualities, such as the sun, moon, and dawn. Figures like Prometheus, Atlas, and Eos play pivotal roles in mythology, contributing to the creation and shaping of humanity and enduring great trials. Their stories highlight themes of sacrifice, endurance, and the ongoing struggle between divine beings and the natural order, demonstrating the continued influence of the Titans even after the rise of the Olympians.

Asteria

Asteria is a Titaness and the daughter of the Titans Coeus and Phoebe. She is associated with the night and the stars, often embodying the celestial phenomena of falling stars and divination through dreams. Asteria is known for her escape from the advances of Zeus by transforming herself into a quail and plunging into the sea, where she became the island of Delos. She is the mother of Hecate, the goddess of magic, witchcraft, and the night, whom she bore with the Titan Perses. Asteria's role in mythology highlights her connection to the stars and the mystical aspects of the night, as well as her significance in the lineage of powerful deities associated with magic and the cosmos.

Astraeus

Astraeus is a Titan associated with the dusk and the stars. He is the son of the Titans Crius and Eurybia. Astraeus married Eos, the goddess of the dawn, and together they had several notable children: the Anemoi (the wind gods, including Boreas, Notus, Eurus, and Zephyrus) and the Astra Planeta (the star gods). Astraeus's role in mythology emphasizes his connection to the celestial and atmospheric phenomena, symbolizing the transition between night and day and the movement of stars and winds. Through his offspring, Astraeus significantly influences the natural world's rhythms and cycles, bridging the gap between the divine and the natural elements.

Atlas

Atlas is a Titan known for his immense strength and endurance. He is the son of the Titans Iapetus and Clymene (or Asia) and is often associated with endurance and astronomy. After the Titans were defeated by the Olympian gods during the Titanomachy, Zeus punished Atlas by condemning him to hold up the sky for eternity. This enduring image of Atlas bearing the celestial sphere on his shoulders symbolizes his role as a pillar of strength and resilience. Beyond this punishment, Atlas is also linked to the world of knowledge and navigation, with ancient maps often adorned with his image. His enduring strength and significant burden have made Atlas a symbol of perseverance and fortitude in the face of overwhelming challenges.

Epimetheus

Epimetheus is a Titan known for his association with afterthought and hindsight. He is the son of the Titans Iapetus and Clymene, and the brother of Prometheus, Atlas, and Menoetius. Unlike his brother Prometheus, who is known for his foresight and wisdom, Epimetheus is characterized by his lack of planning and impulsiveness. He played a crucial role in the myth of Pandora, as he accepted her as his wife despite Prometheus's warnings not to accept any gifts from Zeus. This act led to the release of all the world's evils contained in Pandora's jar (often mistranslated as a box), leaving only hope inside. Epimetheus's story underscores the themes of impulsiveness and the consequences of failing to heed wise counsel.

Eos

Eos is the goddess of the dawn, personifying the first light of day. She is the daughter of the Titans Hyperion and Theia, and the sister of Helios (the Sun) and Selene (the Moon). Eos is often depicted as a beautiful, winged woman who rises from the ocean at the start of each day, bringing light to the world and dispelling the darkness of night. She is known for her many love affairs with both gods and mortals, the most famous being with Tithonus, whom she granted eternal life but not eternal youth, resulting in his endless aging. Eos's role in mythology is essential, as she heralds the arrival of the sun each morning, symbolizing renewal, hope, and the cyclical nature of time.

Helios

Helios is the god and personification of the sun. He is the son of the Titans Hyperion and Theia, and the brother of Selene (the Moon) and Eos (the Dawn). Helios is often depicted as a radiant, handsome god who drives a chariot drawn by four horses across the sky each day, bringing daylight to the world. He begins his journey at dawn, emerging from the ocean in the east, and travels across the heavens before descending into the western sea at dusk. Helios's role is crucial in maintaining the cycle of day and night, and he is revered for his power to illuminate and give life. Though later supplanted by Apollo as the primary sun god in popular worship, Helios remains a significant figure in Greek mythology, embodying the enduring and vital presence of the sun.

Leto

Leto is a Titaness and the daughter of the Titans Coeus and Phoebe. She is primarily known as the mother of the twin Olympian deities Apollo and Artemis, whom she bore with Zeus. Leto's role in mythology is significant as the nurturing and protective mother who, despite facing great adversity, successfully gave birth to her children. Pursued by the jealous Hera, Leto wandered the earth, seeking a safe place to deliver her twins. She eventually found refuge on the floating island of Delos, where she gave birth to Apollo and Artemis. Leto is often depicted as a figure of maternal devotion and resilience, embodying the themes of motherhood and protection. Her story underscores the trials and triumphs of motherhood and the enduring power of a mother's love.

Menoetius

Menoetius is a Titan and the son of Iapetus and Clymene, making him the brother of Prometheus, Epimetheus, and Atlas. Menoetius is often associated with rashness and violent anger, embodying the destructive aspects of human nature. During the Titanomachy, the great war between the Titans and the Olympian gods, Menoetius fought alongside his fellow Titans. However, he was struck down by Zeus for his hubris and violent temperament. As a punishment, Zeus sent Menoetius to Tartarus, the deep abyss used as a dungeon for the Titans. Menoetius's role in mythology serves as a cautionary tale about the dangers of arrogance and uncontrolled rage.

Prometheus

Prometheus is a Titan known for his intelligence and foresight. He is the son of the Titans Iapetus and Clymene and the brother of Epimetheus, Atlas, and Menoetius. Prometheus is most famous for his role as a benefactor to humanity. Defying Zeus, he stole fire from the gods and gifted it to humans, enabling progress and civilization. As punishment for this act of defiance, Zeus had Prometheus bound to a rock where an eagle would eat his liver every day, only for it to regenerate each night, causing him eternal torment. Prometheus's story highlights themes of rebellion, ingenuity, and enduring suffering for the sake of humanity, making him a symbol of resistance against tyranny and a champion of human advancement.

Selene

Selene is the goddess and personification of the Moon. She is the daughter of the Titans Hyperion and Theia, and the sister of Helios (the Sun) and Eos (the Dawn). Selene is often depicted as a beautiful woman with a radiant crown, driving a chariot pulled by two horses across the night sky. Each night, she brings the light of the moon to the world, following her brother Helios's path across the heavens. Selene is also known for her romantic liaison with the mortal Endymion, whom she loved deeply and visited each night as he lay in eternal sleep. Her role in mythology highlights the importance of the moon in the natural cycle, symbolizing beauty, tranquility, and the passage of time.

The Olympians

The Olympians are the most well-known gods in Greek mythology, ruling from their abode on Mount Olympus. They are the direct descendants of the Titans, specifically the children of Cronus and Rhea, and include twelve primary deities such as Zeus, Hera, Poseidon, and Athena. In addition to these twelve, we have included Hades and Dionysus due to their significant roles in Greek mythology. Hades, though he rules the Underworld and does not reside on Olympus, is a brother of Zeus and Poseidon and plays a crucial role in many myths. Dionysus, the god of wine and revelry, is often considered the thirteenth Olympian due to his importance in the pantheon and his frequent inclusion in the myths and stories of the Olympian gods. Together, the Olympian gods govern various aspects of the world and human life, including love, war, wisdom, and the sea. Their myths are central to Greek culture, filled with tales of heroism, betrayal, and the interplay between gods and mortals, and have influenced art, literature, and cultural practices for milennia.

Aphrodite

Aphrodite is the goddess of love, beauty, desire, and fertility. She is one of the twelve Olympian deities and is often depicted as an extraordinarily beautiful and enchanting figure who has the power to ignite passion and affection in both gods and mortals. According to Hesiod's "Theogony," Aphrodite was born from the sea foam that emerged when Cronus severed Uranus's genitals and cast them into the ocean. Another tradition, recounted by Homer in the "Iliad," suggests that she is the daughter of Zeus and the Titaness Dione. Regardless of her origins, Aphrodite's influence is pervasive throughout Greek mythology and culture.

Aphrodite's role in mythology extends beyond her associations with love and beauty. She is also a central figure in many myths and legends. For instance, her affair with Ares, the god of war, highlights the intersection of love and conflict. She is famously linked to the Trojan War, as it was her promise of the most beautiful woman, Helen, to Paris that sparked the conflict. Additionally, Aphrodite played a crucial role in the story of Pygmalion, where she brought a sculptor's ivory statue to life, transforming it into a living woman named Galatea. As the mother of Eros (Cupid), she is intrinsically connected to the concept of romantic love. Aphrodite's dual nature as both a benevolent and potentially destructive force underscores the complex and multifaceted nature of love and desire in human experience. Her worship included various rituals and festivals, celebrating her as a goddess who embodies the profound and irresistible power of attraction and beaut y.

Apollo

Apollo is one of the twelve Olympian deities and is widely revered as the god of the Sun, light, music, poetry, prophecy, healing, and archery. He is the son of Zeus, the king of the gods, and Leto, and the twin brother of Artemis, the goddess of the hunt and the moon. Apollo is often depicted as a handsome, beardless young man with a laurel wreath and a lyre, symbolizing his association with music and the arts. He drives his chariot across the sky, bringing daylight to the world and dispelling darkness.

Apollo's influence and domains are vast and multifaceted. As the god of prophecy, he is associated with the Oracle of Delphi, where his priestess, the Pythia, delivered cryptic predictions and guidance. This oracle was one of the most important religious sites in ancient Greece, drawing visitors from across the Greek world seeking Apollo's divine insight. Apollo is also celebrated for his musical talents, often depicted playing the lyre, and is considered the leader of the Muses, the goddesses of inspiration in literature, science, and the arts.

In addition to his roles in prophecy and the arts, Apollo is a god of healing and medicine. He is the father of Asclepius, the god of medicine, and his associations with health and well-being are evident in various myths where he brings both plague and cure. Apollo's role as an archer is also significant, symbolizing his ability to strike from afar with precision and his role as a protector against evil.

Apollo's mythology includes numerous tales of love, both triumphant and tragic. His pursuit of the nymph Daphne, who transformed into a laurel tree to escape him, is one such story that highlights both his persistence and the complexities of his character. As a god who embodies many aspects of life, Apollo's presence in Greek mythology is profound, representing harmony, order, and the balance between reason and passion. His worship was widespread, and his legacy continues to influence art, culture, and literature to this day.

Ares

Ares is the Olympian god of war, known for his fierce and aggressive nature. He is the son of Zeus, the king of the gods, and Hera, the queen of the gods. Unlike his sister Athena, who represents strategic warfare and wisdom, Ares embodies the brutal and chaotic aspects of conflict. Often depicted as a powerful, battle-ready figure clad in armor and wielding weapons, Ares inspires both fear and respect among gods and mortals alike. His symbols include the spear, helmet, dog, and vulture, all highlighting his martial attributes.

Ares's role in mythology is complex and multifaceted. While he is a formidable force on the battlefield, he is often portrayed in a negative light, embodying the senseless violence and bloodlust of war. His affairs and interactions with other deities further illustrate his tumultuous nature. One of his most famous relationships is with Aphrodite, the goddess of love, despite her being married to Hephaestus, the god of blacksmiths. Their union produced several children, including Eros (Cupid), the god of love, and Harmonia, the goddess of harmony, highlighting the paradoxical connection between love and war.

Despite his fearsome reputation, Ares often faces defeat and humiliation in mythological tales. He is frequently outwitted by other gods and even mortals, such as in the story where he is trapped in a bronze jar by the giants Otus and Ephialtes. His presence in battles, though powerful, is not always decisive or beneficial, reflecting the unpredictable and often destructive nature of war itself.

Ares's worship was less widespread compared to other Olympian gods, with significant cult centers in Sparta and Thrace, where his warlike qualities were particularly revered. His legacy in Greek mythology serves as a reminder of the darker, more chaotic aspects of human conflict, contrasting with the strategic and just nature of Athena's warfare. Through Ares, the Greeks explored the duality of war, acknowledging both its necessity and its potential for destruction.

Artemis

Artemis is one of the twelve Olympian deities and the goddess of the hunt, wilderness, moon, and childbirth. She is the daughter of Zeus, the king of the gods, and Leto, and the twin sister of Apollo, the god of the sun and arts. Artemis is often depicted as a youthful and vigorous huntress, carrying a bow and arrows, accompanied by a pack of hunting dogs or wild animals such as deer. She embodies the untamed and free aspects of nature, symbolizing independence, strength, and the protective spirit of wild places.

Artemis's role in mythology is multifaceted. As the goddess of the hunt, she is the protector of wildlife and the guardian of young animals. She is also associated with the moon, reflecting her dual role alongside her brother Apollo, who governs the sun. In this lunar aspect, Artemis is often depicted wearing a crescent moon on her forehead. Additionally, she is a deity of childbirth and protector of young girls, invoked by women in labor for a safe delivery. Despite her nurturing aspects, Artemis is also known for her fierce and vengeful nature, particularly against those who transgress her boundaries or harm the natural world.

One of the most well-known myths involving Artemis is the story of Actaeon, a hunter who accidentally saw her bathing. In her anger, Artemis transformed him into a stag, and he was subsequently torn apart by his own hunting dogs. This tale underscores her role as a protector of her purity and the sanctity of her chosen domains. Artemis's followers included a group of loyal nymphs, who accompanied her on hunts and shared her commitment to chastity and the wilderness.

Artemis was widely worshipped throughout the Greek world, with significant temples and sanctuaries dedicated to her, such as the Temple of Artemis at Ephesus, one of the Seven Wonders of the Ancient World. Her influence extended beyond Greece, impacting Roman mythology, where she was known as Diana. Artemis's legacy as a powerful, independent, and multifaceted goddess highlights the ancient Greeks' reverence for nature, the wilderness, and the cycles of life and death.

Athena

Athena is one of the twelve Olympian deities and the goddess of wisdom, war, and crafts. She is the daughter of Zeus and Metis, a Titaness known for her wisdom. Athena's birth is unique and dramatic: she sprang fully grown and armored from Zeus's forehead after he swallowed Metis, who was pregnant with her, to prevent a prophecy that her child would be more powerful than its father. Athena is often depicted wearing a helmet and carrying a shield and spear, symbolizing her martial prowess, and is accompanied by an owl, representing wisdom and knowledge.

Athena's role in mythology is multifaceted, encompassing both the strategic aspects of war and the intellectual pursuits of wisdom and crafts. Unlike Ares, who represents the chaotic and violent aspects of conflict, Athena embodies the disciplined and strategic side of warfare, favoring tactics and planning over brute force. She is also the patroness of various crafts, including weaving and pottery, reflecting her connection to practical skills and creativity. Athena's guidance was sought by heroes such as Odysseus, whom she aided during his long journey home in the "Odyssey," and Perseus, whom she helped to defeat the Gorgon Medusa.

One of Athena's most significant contributions to Greek mythology is her role in the founding of the city of Athens, which was named in her honor. According to myth, Athena and Poseidon competed to become the patron deity of the city. Poseidon offered a saltwater spring, while Athena provided the olive tree, symbolizing peace and prosperity. The citizens chose Athena's gift, and the city was named after her, becoming a center of culture, philosophy, and democracy in the ancient world.

Athena's worship was widespread across Greece, with numerous temples and festivals dedicated to her, the most famous being the Parthenon on the Acropolis of Athens. Her legacy as a wise, courageous, and just deity continues to be celebrated in literature, art, and culture. Athena represents the harmonious blend of intellect and strength, embodying the ideal qualities of a leader and protector in Greek mythology.

Demeter

Demeter is one of the twelve Olympian deities and the goddess of agriculture, grain, and fertility. She is the daughter of the Titans Cronus and Rhea and the sister of Zeus, Poseidon, Hades, Hera, and Hestia. Demeter is often depicted with symbols of the harvest, such as sheaves of wheat, a torch, and a cornucopia, reflecting her essential role in sustaining life through the cultivation of crops. Her influence extends to all aspects of agricultural fertility, and she is revered as the nurturer of mankind, ensuring the growth of food and the cycle of the seasons.

One of the most significant myths involving Demeter is the story of her daughter Persephone, whose abduction by Hades to the Underworld caused Demeter profound grief. In her sorrow, Demeter withdrew her blessings from the earth, leading to a barren period where no plants grew, and famine threatened humanity. The plight of the earth only ended when Zeus intervened, and a compromise was reached. Persephone would spend part of the year with Hades in the Underworld, representing the winter months when the earth is barren, and the rest with Demeter, symbolizing the return of spring and the renewal of life. This myth explains the changing seasons and underscores Demeter's deep connection to the cycles of nature and the agricultural calendar.

Demeter's worship was widespread in ancient Greece, with major centers of her cult located at Eleusis, where the Eleusinian Mysteries were held in her honor. These mysteries were among the most important and secretive religious rites in ancient Greece, promising initiates insights into the afterlife and the rebirth of the soul. Demeter's role in mythology emphasizes the vital importance of agriculture and fertility, as well as the profound bond between mother and child. Her influence on Greek culture and religion is profound, symbolizing the sustenance and nurturing aspects of the natural world that are essential for human survival and prosperity.

Dionysus

Dionysus is the god of wine, fertility, revelry, and theater. He is the son of Zeus and the mortal woman Semele, making him one of the few Olympian gods with a mortal parent. Dionysus's birth is marked by drama and divinity: when Semele perished after seeing Zeus in his true form, Zeus saved the unborn Dionysus by sewing him into his thigh until he was ready to be born, making Dionysus "twice-born." Often depicted with grapevines, ivy, and a thyrsus (a staff entwined with ivy and topped with a pine cone), Dionysus embodies the dual nature of joy and chaos, reflecting the intoxicating power of wine and the ecstatic, unpredictable aspects of human experience.

Dionysus's role in Greek mythology is multifaceted and deeply influential. As the god of wine, he is associated with both the pleasures and the dangers of intoxication, symbolizing the liberating and transformative power of alcohol. His followers, including the wild and frenzied Maenads and the satyrs, participated in rites and festivals that celebrated the breaking of societal norms and the embrace of primal instincts. The Dionysian Mysteries, secretive and ecstatic rituals dedicated to Dionysus, promised spiritual release and a closer connection to the divine.

In addition to his association with wine and revelry, Dionysus played a significant role in the development of Greek theater. The City Dionysia, a major festival in Athens held in his honor, featured dramatic competitions that gave rise to some of the greatest works of Greek tragedy and comedy. Dionysus's influence extended to the arts, promoting creativity, emotional expression, and the exploration of human experience through performance.

Dionysus's mythology includes numerous adventures and encounters, such as his journey to the Underworld to rescue his mother Semele and his conquest of India, demonstrating his widespread influence and adventurous spirit. As a god who bridges the gap between the divine and the mortal, the civilized and the wild, Dionysus embodies the complexity of human nature and the transformative power of ecstasy and creativity. His legacy continues to inspire and captivate, highlighting the enduring appeal of liberation, celebration, and artistic expression.

Hades

Hades is the god of the Underworld and the ruler of the realm of the dead. He is the eldest son of the Titans Cronus and Rhea and the brother of Zeus, Poseidon, Hera, Demeter, and Hestia. Unlike his brothers, who ruled the sky and the sea, Hades was given dominion over the Underworld after the defeat of the Titans. Often depicted with a scepter and wearing a helmet of invisibility (the Helm of Darkness), Hades governs a dark and shadowy realm where souls of the deceased reside. Despite his fearsome reputation, Hades is not an evil god; rather, he is a stern but fair ruler who maintains the balance between life and death.

Hades's role in mythology is significant, as he oversees the final resting place of souls and ensures the proper conduct of the dead. His realm is divided into various regions, including the Elysian Fields (a paradise for heroes and the virtuous), the Asphodel Meadows (where ordinary souls dwell), and Tartarus (a place of punishment for the wicked). Hades is also known for his abduction of Persephone, the daughter of Demeter, whom he made his queen. This myth explains the seasonal cycle: Persephone spends part of the year with Hades in the Underworld, causing winter when Demeter mourns her absence, and returns to the surface for the spring and summer, bringing renewal and growth.

While Hades is often associated with death and the afterlife, he is also a god of wealth, due to the precious minerals found underground. This aspect of his character highlights the dual nature of his domain—both the end of life and the source of earthly riches. Hades is less involved in the affairs of the living compared to other gods, but his presence is a constant reminder of the inevitability of death and the importance of the afterlife in Greek culture. His worship was more subdued and less widespread than that of other Olympian deities, but his influence was profound, representing the final boundary every mortal must cross.

Hephaestus

Hephaestus is the god of fire, metalworking, craftsmanship, and volcanoes. He is the son of Zeus and Hera, although some myths suggest that Hera bore him alone in retaliation for Zeus's solo birth of Athena. Unlike the other Olympian gods, Hephaestus is often depicted as physically imperfect, with a pronounced limp due to being thrown from Mount Olympus by Hera or Zeus. Despite his physical limitations, Hephaestus possesses unparalleled skill and creativity, crafting magnificent weapons, armor, and artifacts for gods and heroes alike. He is usually depicted with a hammer and anvil, symbols of his craftsmanship and labor.

Hephaestus's role in mythology is crucial as the divine blacksmith and craftsman. He is credited with creating many famous items, including Hermes's winged sandals, Achilles's armor, and the shield of Heracles. He also forged the chains that bound Prometheus and created Pandora, the first woman, from clay. His forge, often located beneath a volcano, symbolizes the transformative power of fire and metalworking. Hephaestus's creations are not only functional but also imbued with beauty and artistry, reflecting the god's dual nature as both an artisan and a creator.

Despite his significant contributions, Hephaestus's personal life is marked by complexity and conflict. He was married to Aphrodite, the goddess of love and beauty, but their union was troubled by her infidelity with Ares, the god of war. Hephaestus's response to this betrayal involved crafting an unbreakable net to catch the lovers in the act, showcasing both his ingenuity and his emotional depth.

Hephaestus's mythology highlights themes of perseverance, creativity, and the triumph of skill over physical adversity. His workshops, whether in Olympus or beneath the earth, are places of invention and transformation, where raw materials are turned into objects of power and beauty. As the patron of blacksmiths, artisans, and craftsmen, Hephaestus embodies the essential human qualities of hard work, ingenuity, and the ability to create and innovate. His legacy in Greek mythology underscores the importance of craftsmanship and the transformative power of art and technology.

Hera

Hera is the queen of the gods and the goddess of marriage, women, childbirth, and family. She is the daughter of the Titans Cronus and Rhea and the sister and wife of Zeus, the king of the gods. Often depicted as a regal and majestic figure, Hera is usually shown wearing a crown and holding a scepter, symbolizing her authority and status. Her sacred animals include the peacock and the cow, both of which reflect her grandeur and maternal aspects.

Hera's role in mythology is multifaceted and deeply influential. As the goddess of marriage and family, she is the protector of married women and presides over all aspects of matrimony and domestic life. Despite her role as the goddess of marriage, Hera's own marriage to Zeus is notoriously tumultuous, marked by Zeus's numerous infidelities. Hera is often portrayed as jealous and vengeful, directing her wrath not only at Zeus's lovers but also at their offspring. This aspect of her character is evident in the myths of Heracles and Semele, among others, where Hera's jealousy drives the narrative.

Hera's influence extends beyond her marital concerns; she is also a powerful and assertive deity who plays a significant role in various mythological events. In the Iliad, she is a key player in the Trojan War, manipulating events to favor the Greeks. Her strategic and sometimes manipulative nature underscores her capability as a goddess who wields considerable power and influence.

Despite her complex and often contradictory nature, Hera is revered as a protector and nurturer. Her temples, such as the Heraion of Samos and the Heraion of Argos, were important religious centers in ancient Greece. Hera's legacy as the queen of the gods and the embodiment of marriage and family life highlights her enduring importance in Greek mythology and religion. Her stories reflect the complexities of marital relationships and the potent combination of power, jealousy, and maternal devotion.

Hermes

Hermes is the god of commerce, travel, communication, and cunning. He is the son of Zeus and the nymph Maia, making him one of the twelve Olympian deities. Hermes is often depicted as a youthful and athletic figure with winged sandals and a winged helmet, symbolizing his role as the swift messenger of the gods. He carries a caduceus, a staff entwined with two serpents, which represents his authority and his role as a guide for souls to the Underworld.

Hermes's role in mythology is diverse and multifaceted. As the herald of the gods, he is responsible for conveying messages and conducting the will of Zeus. His speed and mobility make him the ideal intermediary, capable of moving freely between the divine, mortal, and Underworld realms. Hermes is also the god of boundaries and transitions, overseeing travelers, merchants, and thieves. His cunning and resourcefulness are evident in numerous myths, such as the story of his invention of the lyre from a tortoise shell and his clever theft of Apollo's cattle as an infant, which he later reconciled by gifting Apollo the lyre.

In addition to his role as a messenger and guide, Hermes is the protector of commerce and trade. He is associated with market activities, bringing good fortune and prosperity to those who honor him. His influence extends to language and rhetoric, making him a patron of eloquence and persuasive speech. Hermes is also known for his role as a psychopomp, guiding the souls of the dead to the Underworld, ensuring their safe passage.

Hermes's worship was widespread in ancient Greece, with numerous temples and shrines dedicated to him. His attributes of swiftness, cunning, and versatility made him a beloved and relatable deity, embodying the dynamic and unpredictable aspects of life. Hermes's legacy in mythology and culture highlights the importance of communication, adaptability, and the ability to navigate complex situations with skill and ingenuity.

Hestia

Hestia is the goddess of the hearth, home, and domestic life. She is the eldest daughter of the Titans Cronus and Rhea, and the sister of Zeus, Hera, Poseidon, Demeter, and Hades. Hestia is often depicted as a modestly veiled woman, symbolizing her serene and unassuming nature. As the goddess of the hearth, she presides over the household fire, which was central to both daily life and religious practices in ancient Greece. Her role extends to the protection of the family, ensuring harmony and warmth within the home.

Hestia's influence is significant despite her quiet and often understated presence in mythology. She is revered as the embodiment of domestic stability and hospitality, and every home and temple had a hearth dedicated to her. As a virgin goddess, she embodies purity and the sanctity of the domestic sphere. Hestia's commitment to maintaining peace and order within the household reflects her broader role in preserving social and familial unity.

Hestia is also central to public worship and community life. In city-states across Greece, the prytaneion (the public hearth) was dedicated to her, and her flame was kept perpetually burning as a symbol of communal well-being and continuity. When new colonies were established, a flame from Hestia's hearth in the mother city was carried to the new settlement to ensure its prosperity and connection to its origins. Despite her vital role, Hestia willingly gave up her seat among the twelve Olympians to Dionysus, preferring to remain more closely connected to the daily lives of mortals. Her legacy underscores the importance of home, family, and communal harmony in Greek culture, making her one of the most universally respected and beloved deities in the Greek pantheon.

Poseidon

Poseidon is the powerful god of the sea, earthquakes, and horses. He is one of the twelve Olympian deities and the son of the Titans Cronus and Rhea. As the brother of Zeus, the king of the gods, and Hades, the ruler of the Underworld, Poseidon holds dominion over all waters, both salt and freshwater. He is typically depicted as a mature, bearded man wielding a trident, his signature weapon, which he uses to control the seas and unleash his wrath upon those who anger h im.

Poseidon's role in mythology is extensive and multifaceted. As the god of the sea, he is worshipped by sailors and fishermen who seek his favor for safe voyages and bountiful catches. His influence extends to the creation and control of storms, making him both a protector and a formidable adversary to those who travel by sea. Poseidon's ability to cause earthquakes earned him the epithet "Earth-shaker," reflecting his power over the land as well as the sea. This dual control highlights his volatile nature, capable of both nurturing and destruction.

In addition to his dominion over natural elements, Poseidon is associated with horses, often credited with creating the first horse and inspiring the domestication and breeding of these animals. He is also involved in numerous myths, such as the contest with Athena for the patronage of Athens, which he lost after offering a saltwater spring while Athena provided an olive tree. Despite this loss, Poseidon remained a highly revered deity throughout Greece, with major temples such as the one at Cape Sounion dedicated to his worship.

Poseidon's numerous romantic escapades and offspring, both mortal and divine, further illustrate his far-reaching influence. His children include the hero Theseus, the Cyclops Polyphemus, and the sea god Triton. Poseidon's complex character, embodying both the nurturing aspects of water and the destructive power of natural disasters, makes him a central figure in Greek mythology. His worship reflects the ancient Greeks' deep respect for the sea's vital yet unpredictable nature, acknowledging Poseidon's crucial role in their world.

Zeus

Zeus is the king of the gods and the ruler of Mount Olympus. He is the youngest son of the Titans Cronus and Rhea and is known for his supreme authority over the sky and thunder. Zeus is often depicted as a regal, mature man with a sturdy figure, holding a lightning bolt, his most powerful weapon. His symbols also include the eagle, the oak tree, and the throne, representing his dominance and sovereignty over both the divine and mortal realms.

Zeus's rise to power is marked by a dramatic narrative of rebellion and triumph. To avoid being swallowed by his father, Cronus, who feared a prophecy that one of his children would overthrow him, Rhea hid the newborn Zeus in a cave on the island of Crete. Upon reaching adulthood, Zeus led a successful revolt against Cronus and the Titans, freeing his siblings and establishing the rule of the Olympian gods. This victory cemented his position as the supreme deity and protector of law, order, and justice.

As the king of the gods, Zeus presides over the pantheon, maintaining order and ensuring the stability of the cosmos. His role encompasses various aspects of life, including governance, weather, and fate. Zeus is often involved in the affairs of mortals and gods alike, mediating disputes and enforcing divine laws. Despite his just and noble nature, Zeus is also known for his numerous romantic escapades, resulting in a myriad of offspring, both mortal and divine. These relationships highlight his complex character, blending authority with human-like flaws and desires.

Zeus's influence extends to many myths and legends, such as his role in the Trojan War, where he attempts to maintain a balance between the warring sides, and his numerous heroic progeny, including Hercules and Perseus. His worship was widespread in ancient Greece, with major sanctuaries like Olympia and Dodona dedicated to him. Zeus's legacy as the god of the sky and thunder, the arbiter of justice, and the patriarch of gods and heroes, underscores his pivotal role in Greek mythology and his enduring symbol of power and authority.

CHAPTER 2: HEROES, DEMI-GODS, AND LEGENDARY FIGURES

In this chapter, we explore the prominent heroes, demi-gods, and legendary figures who play crucial roles in Greek mythology. These characters are listed in alphabetical order for ease of reference, providing a brief overview of their stories, attributes, and significance. Whether you choose to read this chapter in its entirety to familiarize yourself with these legendary figures, or prefer to refer to it as you encounter them in the myths, this section serves as a valuable resource for understanding the rich tapestry of Greek mythology. Here, you will find the tales of mighty warriors, cunning adventurers, and tragic heroes whose exploits and legacies have shaped the ancient Greek world and continue to captivate us today.

Achilles

Achilles is one of the greatest heroes in Greek mythology, known for his unmatched prowess as a warrior in the Trojan War. He is the son of Peleus, a mortal king, and Thetis, a sea nymph, making him both mortal and divine. According to myth, Thetis dipped Achilles in the River Styx as an infant, rendering him invulnerable except for his heel, where she held him—a vulnerability that would later lead to his death. Achilles is the central character in Homer's Iliad, where his rage and withdrawal from battle significantly influence the course of the war. His role in mythology is marked by his extraordinary strength, bravery, and tragic fate, highlighting themes of heroism, mortality, and the quest for glory.

Adonis

Adonis is a handsome youth associated with beauty, desire, and the cycle of life and death. He is the son of Myrrha (or Smyrna) and her father, King Cinyras, conceived through divine intervention or trickery, depending on the version of the myth. Adonis's extraordinary beauty captivated both Aphrodite, the goddess of love, and Persephone, the queen of the Underworld, leading to a conflict over him. Eventually, Zeus decreed that Adonis would spend part of the year with Aphrodite and part with Persephone, symbolizing the seasonal cycle of growth and decay. Adonis's myth is closely linked to themes of love, beauty, and the natural cycles of renewal and decline, making him a significant figure in ancient fertility cults and rituals.

Aeneas

Aeneas is a Trojan hero and the son of the goddess Aphrodite and the mortal prince Anchises. He plays a crucial role in both Greek and Roman mythology, particularly in the epic tale of the Aeneid by the Roman poet Virgil. Aeneas is one of the few Trojans to survive the fall of Troy, and he is destined to become the ancestor of the Romans. Guided by his divine mother and other gods, Aeneas leads a group of survivors on a perilous journey to Italy, where he is fated to lay the foundations for what will become Rome. His character embodies piety, duty, and perseverance, making him a symbol of Roman virtues and the ideal hero who balances personal sacrifice with the greater good of founding a new civilization.

Ajax the Great

Ajax the Great is a towering warrior and hero of the Trojan War, known for his immense strength, courage, and loyalty. He is the son of Telamon, king of Salamis, and a nephew of Peleus, making him a cousin of Achilles. Ajax is often depicted as a giant of a man, wielding a massive shield that protects not only himself but also his comrades in battle. In Homer's Iliad, Ajax is one of the most formidable Greek warriors, second only to Achilles in combat prowess. He plays a crucial role in defending the Greek ships from the Trojans and duels with Hector, the Trojan prince, in a famous but inconclusive battle.

Ajax's story takes a tragic turn after the death of Achilles. When Achilles's armor is awarded to Odysseus instead of him, Ajax, feeling dishonored and enraged, falls into a deep despair. In his grief-stricken madness, he slaughters a herd of livestock, mistaking them for his enemies. Upon realizing his actions, Ajax is overcome with shame and takes his own life. His tragic end highlights themes of pride, honor, and the devastating effects of war on even the mightiest of heroes. Ajax the Great is remembered as a symbol of unyielding strength and tragic nobility in Greek mythology.

Andromeda

Andromeda is a princess known for her beauty and her dramatic rescue by the hero Perseus. She is the daughter of King Cepheus and Queen Cassiopeia of Ethiopia. Andromeda's story begins when her mother, Cassiopeia, boasts that Andromeda is more beautiful than the Nereids, the sea nymphs. Offended by this hubris, Poseidon, the god of the sea, sends a sea monster to ravage the coast of Ethiopia. To appease the god and save their kingdom, Cepheus and Cassiopeia are forced to sacrifice Andromeda by chaining her to a rock as an offering to the monster.

As Andromeda awaits her fate, Perseus, returning from his quest to slay Medusa, spots her and is struck by her beauty. He bravely confronts and defeats the sea monster, saving Andromeda and winning her hand in marriage. Their union is blessed, and Andromeda becomes an important figure in Perseus's later adventures. After her death, Andromeda is immortalized among the stars as a constellation, reflecting her lasting significance in Greek mythology. Her story is often seen as a tale of sacrifice, redemption, and the triumph of heroism over adversity.

Atalanta

Atalanta is a renowned heroine known for her exceptional speed, strength, and independence. She was abandoned at birth by her father, who desired a son, and was raised by a she-bear and later by hunters, which shaped her into a skilled huntress and warrior. Atalanta is best known for her participation in the Calydonian Boar Hunt, where she was the first to wound the monstrous boar, earning the respect and admiration of her fellow hunters.

Atalanta's other famous tale involves her suitors. Determined to remain unmarried, she challenged her potential husbands to a footrace, promising to marry only the man who could outrun her. However, Atalanta was so swift that none could defeat her until Hippomenes, with the help of the goddess Aphrodite, tricked her by dropping three golden apples during the race. Atalanta paused to pick them up, allowing Hippomenes to win and claim her hand in marriage. Despite her reluctant marriage, Atalanta remained a symbol of strength, athleticism, and the power of women in a predominantly male-dominated mythology. Her story reflects themes of independence, the challenges of love, and the struggle to balance personal freedom with societal expectations.

Bellerophon

Bellerophon is a celebrated hero known for taming the winged horse Pegasus and defeating the fearsome Chimera, a fire-breathing monster with the body of a lion, the head of a goat, and the tail of a serpent. He is the son of the Corinthian king Glaucus (or, in some accounts, the god Poseidon) and is often depicted as a noble and courageous figure.

Bellerophon's most famous exploit begins when he is sent on a seemingly impossible mission to kill the Chimera, a task intended to lead to his death. However, with the aid of the goddess Athena, who helps him tame Pegasus, Bellerophon is able to fly above the Chimera and slay the beast from the air, using a spear or arrows. This victory cements his reputation as one of Greece's greatest heroes.

Despite his successes, Bellerophon's story takes a tragic turn due to his hubris. He attempts to fly Pegasus to Mount Olympus, the home of the gods, but Zeus, angered by his arrogance, sends a gadfly to sting Pegasus, causing the horse to throw Bellerophon off. He falls back to Earth, surviving but living the rest of his days in misery and isolation. Bellerophon's tale serves as a cautionary story about the dangers of overreaching and the consequences of pride.

Cadmus

Cadmus is a legendary hero and the founder of the city of Thebes. He is the son of Agenor, the king of Tyre, and the brother of Europa. Cadmus is most famous for his quest to find his sister Europa after she was abducted by Zeus. When his search proved fruitless, the Oracle of Delphi advised him to cease his search and instead follow a special cow until it lay down, where he was to found a city. This led him to establish Thebes in the region of Boeotia.

One of Cadmus's most significant myths involves his encounter with a dragon, sacred to Ares, which guarded a spring near Thebes. After slaying the dragon, Cadmus was instructed by Athena to sow its teeth into the ground. From these teeth sprang a group of fierce warriors known as the Spartoi. To secure peace, Cadmus threw a stone among them, causing them to fight one another until only five remained. These five survivors became the ancestors of Theban nobility.

Cadmus's role in mythology is also marked by his marriage to Harmonia, the daughter of Ares and Aphrodite, which was one of the most celebrated unions in Greek mythology. However, his life was not without tragedy, as he and Harmonia later faced numerous misfortunes, including the eventual downfall of their descendants. Cadmus is often remembered as a wise and resilient figure who brought civilization to Thebes and introduced the Phoenician alphabet to Greece, laying the foundation for Greek literacy.

Daedalus

Daedalus is a brilliant inventor, architect, and craftsman, renowned for his unparalleled ingenuity. He is credited with designing the labyrinth on the island of Crete, a vast and complex maze created to house the Minotaur, a monstrous creature that was half-man, half-bull. Daedalus is also known for his role in the myth of Icarus, his son. When King Minos of Crete imprisoned Daedalus and Icarus to prevent the secret of the labyrinth from spreading, Daedalus fashioned wings made of feathers and wax for their escape.

Daedalus's warning to Icarus—to fly neither too high, where the sun's heat would melt the wax, nor too low, where the sea's dampness would weigh down the wings—was tragically ignored. Icarus, overcome with exhilaration, flew too close to the sun, causing the wax to melt, and he fell into the sea and drowned. This story highlights Daedalus's role as both a loving father and a symbol of human ingenuity and the dangers of hubris. Beyond the tale of Icarus, Daedalus is also associated with various other inventions and contributions to art and architecture in Greek mythology, solidifying his legacy as one of the most talented and resourceful figures in ancient lore.

Diomedes

Diomedes is a prominent Greek hero and king of Argos, best known for his valiant role in the Trojan War. He is the son of Tydeus, one of the famed Seven Against Thebes, and Deipyle. Diomedes is one of the leading warriors in Homer's Iliad, renowned for his courage, intelligence, and martial prowess. In the epic, he is often depicted as second only to Achilles in bravery and strength.

One of Diomedes's most famous exploits during the Trojan War is his daring night raid with Odysseus, during which they infiltrate the Trojan camp and kill the Thracian king Rhesus, capturing his prized horses. Diomedes also plays a crucial role in several key battles, including wounding the gods Ares and Aphrodite on the battlefield, a testament to his extraordinary valor and divine favor. Diomedes is characterized by his piety, wisdom, and leadership, and after the war, he is one of the few Greek heroes who return home safely, continuing his reign in Argos. His story reflects the ideals of heroism and the complex interplay between mortals and gods in Greek mythology.

Hector

Hector is the eldest son of King Priam and Queen Hecuba of Troy and the greatest warrior of the Trojan army during the Trojan War. As the prince of Troy, Hector is a central figure in Homer's Iliad, where he is depicted as a noble and courageous leader who fights to protect his city and family. Unlike many Greek heroes, Hector is not driven by personal glory but by his sense of duty and love for his homeland and loved ones.

Hector's role in the Trojan War is pivotal, as he leads the defense of Troy against the invading Greek forces. He is portrayed as a compassionate and honorable warrior, deeply devoted to his wife Andromache and their young son, Astyanax. Hector's most famous battle is his duel with Achilles, the greatest of the Greek warriors. Despite knowing that he is fated to die, Hector faces Achilles with bravery, ultimately falling in combat. His death marks a turning point in the war and symbolizes the inevitable fall of Troy.

Hector is remembered as a paragon of the heroic virtues of bravery, loyalty, and selflessness. His character contrasts with the often more individualistic Greek heroes, highlighting the themes of honor, sacrifice, and the tragic consequences of war. Hector's legacy endures as one of the most poignant and respected figures in Greek mythology.

Helen of Troy

Helen of Troy is renowned as the most beautiful woman in the world and a central figure in the events leading to the Trojan War. She is the daughter of Zeus and Leda, making her semi-divine, and the sister of Castor, Pollux, and Clytemnestra. Helen was originally the queen of Sparta, married to King Menelaus. However, her elopement (or abduction, according to some versions) with Paris, the prince of Troy, sparked the legendary conflict between the Greeks and Trojans.

Helen's role in mythology is both pivotal and complex. She is often portrayed as a figure of immense beauty whose very presence could incite war and destruction. Her departure from Sparta to Troy is seen as the catalyst for the ten-year Trojan War, as Menelaus and the Greek kings, bound by an oath, launched a massive expedition to retrieve her, leading to one of the most famous conflicts in literature. Throughout the Iliad and other works, Helen is depicted with varying degrees of sympathy—sometimes as a willing participant in the events, other times as a pawn of the gods.

Heracles

Heracles, also known as Hercules in Roman mythology, is one of the most celebrated heroes in Greek mythology, renowned for his incredible strength, courage, and endurance. He is the son of Zeus, the king of the gods, and Alcmene, a mortal woman, making him a demigod with extraordinary abilities. Heracles is best known for the Twelve Labors, a series of nearly impossible tasks he was compelled to complete as penance for killing his wife and children in a fit of madness caused by Hera, Zeus's jealous wife.

Each labor tested Heracles's physical and mental strength, ranging from slaying the Nemean Lion and capturing the Golden Hind of Artemis to retrieving the Apples of the Hesperides and capturing Cerberus, the guard dog of the Underworld. These labors not only demonstrate his superhuman capabilities but also his resilience and determination to atone for his actions and achieve redemption.

Heracles's role in mythology extends beyond his labors. He is a complex figure who embodies both the noble and flawed aspects of heroism. Despite his divine lineage, Heracles often faced immense suffering and challenges, reflecting the human condition's trials. His character represents the ideal of heroism in Greek culture, combining physical might with moral fortitude, and his legacy has endured as a symbol of strength and perseverance throughout the centuries.

Icarus

Icarus is the son of the master craftsman Daedalus, who is famous for his role in the story of the Labyrinth and the Minotaur. Icarus is best known for the tragic tale of his ill-fated flight. To escape from the island of Crete, where they were imprisoned by King Minos, Daedalus constructed two sets of wings made of feathers and wax for himself and Icarus. Before taking off, Daedalus warned his son not to fly too close to the sun or too close to the sea—flying too high would melt the wax, while flying too low would cause the wings to become damp and heavy.

Overcome with the exhilaration of flight, Icarus ignored his father's warnings and soared higher and higher. As he flew too close to the sun, the wax in his wings melted, causing him to plummet into the sea where he drowned. This story is often interpreted as a cautionary tale about the dangers of hubris, overconfidence, and the consequences of not heeding wise advice. Icarus's fall symbolizes the perils of excessive ambition and the fragile balance between aspiration and recklessness. His tragic fate has become a powerful metaphor for human overreach and the limits of ambition.

Jason

Jason is a hero best known for leading the Argonauts on the quest for the Golden Fleece, a journey filled with peril and adventure. He is the son of Aeson, the rightful king of Iolcus, and was raised by the centaur Chiron after his uncle Pelias usurped the throne. Jason's most famous myth begins when he returns to Iolcus to claim his rightful place as king. Pelias agrees to relinquish the throne if Jason can bring him the Golden Fleece, a powerful and magical artifact guarded by a dragon in the distant land of Colchis.

Jason assembles a crew of heroes, known as the Argonauts, and sets sail on the ship Argo. His journey is marked by numerous challenges, including encounters with harpies, clashing rocks, and the sorceress Medea, who falls in love with him and helps him secure the fleece through her magic. With Medea's assistance, Jason succeeds in obtaining the Golden Fleece and returns to Iolcus, but his story does not end there. Jason's later life is marred by tragedy and betrayal, particularly his abandonment of Medea, which leads to a series of catastrophic events.

Medea

Medea is a powerful sorceress and the daughter of King Aeëtes of Colchis, and the granddaughter of the sun god Helios. She is best known for her role in the myth of Jason and the Argonauts, where she falls deeply in love with Jason and uses her magical abilities to help him secure the Golden Fleece. Medea's love for Jason drives her to betray her own family, including helping Jason overcome the tasks set by her father and ultimately fleeing with him back to Greece.

Medea's story takes a darker turn after Jason abandons her to marry Glauce, the daughter of the king of Corinth, in pursuit of power and status. In a fit of vengeance and betrayal, Medea enacts a horrific revenge, killing Glauce, her father, and, in some versions of the myth, even her own children by Jason to inflict the deepest possible pain on him. Medea's actions have made her one of the most complex and controversial figures in Greek mythology, embodying themes of love, betrayal, revenge, and the extremes of human emotion. Her story explores the consequences of passion and the darker side of the human psyche, making her a tragic and enduring figure in classical literature.

Odysseus

Odysseus is the king of Ithaca and one of the most cunning and resourceful heroes of the Trojan War. He is the central character in Homer's epic, The Odyssey, which recounts his long and arduous journey home after the fall of Troy. Known for his intelligence, eloquence, and strategic mind, Odysseus played a crucial role in the Greek victory during the Trojan War, most famously devising the plan of the Trojan Horse, which led to the fall of Troy.

Odysseus's journey home to Ithaca is marked by numerous trials and adventures, including encounters with the Cyclops Polyphemus, the Sirens, the sorceress Circe, and the nymph Calypso, who detains him on her island for several years. Despite these challenges, Odysseus remains determined to return to his wife, Penelope, and son, Telemachus. His journey symbolizes the human struggle against adversity, the longing for home, and the importance of cleverness and re-silience in overcoming obstacles. Odysseus's character embodies the Greek virtues of intelligence, bravery, and perseverance, making him one of the most enduring and celebrated heroes in Greek mythology.

Oedipus

Oedipus is a tragic hero best known for his role in the Theban plays by Sophocles, particularly Oedipus Rex. He is the son of King Laius and Queen Jocasta of Thebes. According to prophecy, Oedipus was destined to kill his father and marry his mother. To prevent this, his parents abandoned him as an infant, but he was rescued and raised by the king and queen of Corinth.

Unaware of his true identity, Oedipus later leaves Corinth to avoid fulfilling the prophecy, only to unknowingly kill his real father, Laius, in a chance encounter. He then solves the riddle of the Sphinx, which had been terrorizing Thebes, and is rewarded with the throne and the hand of the widowed queen, Jocasta—his mother. When the truth of his actions is eventually revealed, Oedipus is horrified and blinds himself in despair, while Jocasta takes her own life.

Orpheus

Orpheus is a legendary musician, poet, and prophet known for his extraordinary ability to charm all living things—and even inanimate objects—with his music. He is the son of the muse Calliope and either the god Apollo or the Thracian king Oeagrus. Orpheus is most famous for his tragic love story with Eurydice. After Eurydice dies from a snake bite, Orpheus, stricken with grief, journeys to the Underworld to bring her back. Using the power of his enchanting music, he softens the hearts of Hades and Persephone, who agree to let Eurydice return to the living world on the condition that Orpheus does not look back at her until they have both reached the surface.

Tragically, just as they are about to exit the Underworld, Orpheus, overcome with doubt and anxiety, turns to look at Eurydice, causing her to vanish forever. This story underscores themes of love, loss, and the limitations of human frailty. Orpheus's myth has inspired countless works of art, literature, and music, symbolizing the power of art and the profound sorrow that can accompany love. Orpheus's legacy also includes his association with the Orphic mysteries, religious rites that focused on the afterlife and the soul's immortality.

Pandora

Pandora is the first mortal woman, created by the gods as part of a divine punishment for humanity. She was fashioned by Hephaestus on the orders of Zeus, who sought to counteract the blessing of fire that Prometheus had stolen from the gods and given to humans. Each god contributed a gift to Pandora, endowing her with beauty, charm, and cunning, but also with a deceptive nature. She is best known for the myth of Pandora's Box (originally a jar), which she was given but instructed not to open.

Overcome by curiosity, Pandora eventually opened the jar, releasing all the evils—such as disease, sorrow, and death—into the world, leaving only Hope trapped inside when she quickly closed it again. This myth explains the origin of human suffering and the dual nature of existence, where both hope and despair coexist. Pandora's story is a cautionary tale about the dangers of curiosity and the unintended consequences of disobedience, marking her as a pivotal figure in the ancient Greek understanding of human nature and the origin of life's hardships.

Paris

Paris is a prince of Troy and the son of King Priam and Queen Hecuba. He is best known for his role in sparking the Trojan War. Before his birth, it was prophesied that Paris would be the cause of Troy's destruction, leading his parents to abandon him on Mount Ida. However, he was rescued and raised by shepherds, unaware of his royal lineage.

Paris's most famous act is his involvement in the Judgment of Paris, a contest among the goddesses Hera, Athena, and Aphrodite to determine the fairest. Each goddess offered Paris a bribe: Hera promised power, Athena offered wisdom and victory in battle, and Aphrodite promised the most beautiful woman in the world. Paris awarded the golden apple to Aphrodite, who in return helped him win the love of Helen, the wife of King Menelaus of Sparta. Paris's abduction (or elopement) of Helen led to the Greek expedition to Troy, igniting the Trojan War.

Throughout the war, Paris is depicted as a skilled archer but also as a somewhat passive figure, often overshadowed by the heroics of his brother Hector and others. His actions, driven by love and divine influence, ultimately fulfill the prophecy of Troy's downfall, making him a central yet tragic figure in the epic cycle of the Trojan War.

Patroclus

Patroclus is a close companion and beloved friend of Achilles, the greatest Greek warrior in the Trojan War. He is the son of Menoetius and was raised alongside Achilles in the court of King Peleus, where they developed a deep bond that is central to the Iliad. Patroclus is portrayed as loyal, compassionate, and a skilled warrior in his own right.

During the Trojan War, when Achilles withdraws from battle after a dispute with Agamemnon, the Greek forces begin to falter. Desperate to turn the tide, Patroclus dons Achilles's armor and leads the Myrmidons into battle, successfully driving the Trojans back. However, in his bravery, Patroclus pushes too far and is ultimately killed by Hector, the Trojan prince. His death becomes the catalyst for Achilles's return to the battlefield, driven by grief and rage, leading to some of the most dramatic and tragic events in the Iliad.

Patroclus's death highlights the themes of friendship, loyalty, and the tragic consequences of war. His relationship with Achilles is one of the most poignant in Greek mythology, underscoring the deep emotional bonds that drive the epic's narrative.

Perseus

Perseus is a celebrated hero best known for slaying the Gorgon Medusa, whose gaze could turn anyone to stone. He is the son of Zeus, the king of the gods, and

Danaë, a mortal princess. Perseus's birth itself is extraordinary, as his grandfather, King Acrisius of Argos, tried to prevent it by locking Danaë in a bronze chamber, but Zeus entered as a shower of gold, impregnating her. Fearing a prophecy that her son would kill him, Acrisius set Danaë and the infant Perseus adrift at sea, but they survived and were rescued by a fisherman.

Perseus's most famous adventure is his quest to obtain the head of Medusa, one of the three Gorgons. With the help of divine gifts, including a mirrored shield from Athena, winged sandals from Hermes, and a sword from Hephaestus, Perseus successfully beheads Medusa by looking at her reflection in the shield to avoid being turned to stone. He later uses Medusa's head as a weapon, turning his enemies to stone, and performs other heroic deeds, such as rescuing the princess Andromeda from a sea monster and eventually marrying her.

Perseus's story highlights themes of bravery, cleverness, and divine favor. He is considered one of the greatest Greek heroes, and his exploits laid the foundations for later myths and legends, including the establishment of the city of Mycenae. Perseus's adventures also emphasize the importance of fate, as his actions ultimately fulfill the prophecy that he would inadvertently cause his grandfather's death, despite all efforts to avoid it.

Prometheus

Prometheus, in Greek mythology, is a Titan known for his intelligence, foresight, and compassion for humanity. He is the son of the Titan Iapetus and the Oceanid Clymene, and the brother of Epimetheus, Atlas, and Menoetius. Prometheus is most famous for defying Zeus, the king of the gods, by stealing fire from the heavens and giving it to humans, enabling them to develop civilization, technology, and warmth. This act of rebellion symbolizes Prometheus's role as a benefactor of humanity, as he sought to elevate humans from their primitive state.

As punishment for his defiance, Zeus had Prometheus bound to a rock in the Caucasus Mountains, where an eagle would devour his liver every day, only for it to regenerate each night, subjecting him to eternal torment. Prometheus's suffering continued until he was eventually freed by the hero Heracles.

Sisyphus

Sisyphus is a cunning and deceitful king of Corinth known for his intelligence and trickery, which he used to defy the gods. He is infamous for repeatedly cheating death, most notably by twice escaping from the Underworld. In one version of the myth, Sisyphus traps Thanatos, the personification of death, preventing anyone from dying until Ares intervenes. In another tale, he convinces Persephone to allow him to return to the living world after his death by claiming he needed to punish his wife for not performing the proper burial rites.

As punishment for his hubris and defiance of the gods, Zeus condemned Sisyphus to an eternity of futile labor in the Underworld. His eternal punishment was to roll a massive boulder up a hill, only for it to roll back down each time he neared the summit, forcing him to start the task all over again. This endless and meaningless toil has made Sisyphus a symbol of futility and the human condition, representing the struggle against inevitable defeat.

Theseus

Theseus is a legendary hero and the king of Athens, celebrated for his many adventures and heroic deeds. He is the son of Aegeus, the king of Athens, and Aethra, although some myths suggest that he is also the son of Poseidon, the god of the sea. Theseus is best known for his journey to Crete, where he entered the labyrinth and defeated the Minotaur, a monstrous creature with the body of a man and the head of a bull. He successfully navigated the labyrinth with the help of Ariadne, the daughter of King Minos, who gave him a ball of thread to trace his path back out.

Theseus's role in mythology extends beyond his victory over the Minotaur. He is credited with unifying the city of Athens, establishing it as a powerful city-state, and implementing democratic reforms. Theseus is also known for his adventures with the Amazons, where he abducted their queen, Hippolyta, and for his friendship with Pirithous, with whom he undertook various daring quests. His later life was marked by tragedy and misfortune, including the death of his son Hippolytus and his own eventual exile and death.

CHAPTER 3: MONSTERS AND MYTHICAL CREATURES

In this chapter, we delve into the fascinating world of monsters and mythical creatures that inhabit Greek mythology. These beings, often representing chaos, fear, and the unknown, play pivotal roles in the adventures and trials faced by the heroes and gods. Listed in alphabetical order for ease of reference, each entry provides a glimpse into their origins, characteristics, and the legends that surround them. Whether you read this chapter sequentially to immerse yourself in the diverse array of creatures or use it as a reference while exploring the myths, this section offers valuable insights into the formidable and fantastical beings that add depth and excitement to Greek mythology. From fearsome beasts like the Minotaur to enigmatic entities like the Sphinx, these creatures challenge and intrigue, highlighting the bravery and ingenuity of those who confront them.

Arachne

Arachne is a talented mortal weaver who becomes the central figure in a cautionary tale about pride and hubris. She was renowned for her exceptional skill in weaving, so much so that she boldly claimed she was a better weaver than Athena, the goddess of wisdom and crafts. Offended by this claim, Athena challenged Arachne to a weaving contest.

Arachne's tapestry depicted the gods in unflattering ways, particularly their many misdeeds and infidelities, while Athena wove scenes of the gods in their majesty. Though Arachne's work was flawless, her hubris in challenging a goddess led to her downfall. In anger or pity (depending on the version of the myth), Athena transformed Arachne into a spider, condemning her to weave for eternity.

Arachne's story serves as a warning against excessive pride and the dangers of challenging the gods, illustrating the consequences of overestimating one's abilities and disrespecting divine authority. Her transformation into a spider explains the origin of spiders and their webs, and the myth has become a symbolic lesson on humility and the limits of human ambition.

Argus

Argus is a giant known as Argus Panoptes, which means "Argus the All-Seeing." He is famous for having a hundred eyes, which made him an excellent watchman, as he could keep many of his eyes open while others slept. Argus was a loyal servant of the goddess Hera, who entrusted him with various tasks, most notably guarding Io, a nymph whom Zeus had transformed into a cow to hide her from Hera's jealousy. Argus's role was to keep Io under constant surveillance, preventing Zeus from rescuing her.

To free Io, Zeus sent Hermes to deal with Argus. Hermes used his cunning and played soothing music on his lyre, lulling all of Argus's eyes to sleep. Once Argus was completely asleep, Hermes killed him, thus freeing Io. To honor her faithful servant, Hera placed Argus's hundred eyes on the tail of the peacock, which became the bird's most distinctive feature.

Argus's story is a tale of loyalty and vigilance, and his many eyes symbolize his ability to see and know more than any other being, reinforcing his role as a formidable guardian in Greek mythology.

Cerberus

Cerberus is the fearsome three-headed dog that guards the entrance to the Underworld, preventing the dead from leaving and the living from entering without permission. He is the offspring of the monstrous giants Typhon and Echidna, making him one of several terrifying creatures in Greek mythology. Each of Cerberus's three heads is said to represent the past, present, and future, and he also has a serpent's tail and snakes protruding from various parts of his body, adding to his terrifying appearance.

Cerberus plays a crucial role in maintaining the boundaries of the Underworld, serving as Hades' loyal guardian. One of the most famous myths involving Cerberus is the twelfth labor of Heracles, in which the hero is tasked with capturing Cerberus and bringing him to the surface world without using weapons. Heracles successfully accomplishes this feat, showcasing his incredible strength and courage.

Cerberus is a symbol of the inescapable nature of death and the formidable barriers between the world of the living and the dead. His image has endured as a powerful representation of the Underworld's impenetrable defenses and the concept of mortality in Greek mythology.

Charybdis

Charybdis is a monstrous sea creature known for creating deadly whirlpools that could swallow entire ships. She is often depicted as a giant mouth or vortex in the sea, and her insatiable thirst causes her to drink down vast amounts of water and then spew it back out, creating massive whirlpools. Charybdis is one of the two sea hazards that sailors must navigate between, the other being Scylla, a six-headed monster, in the narrow strait of Messina.

Charybdis plays a crucial role in Homer's Odyssey, where the hero Odysseus must choose between risking his ship and crew by passing too close to either Charybdis or Scylla. He ultimately decides to sail closer to Scylla, believing it better to lose a few men than to risk his entire ship being swallowed by Charybdis's whirlpool. The myth of Charybdis emphasizes the dangers of the sea and the perilous decisions that sailors must make, often symbolizing unavoidable dangers and the concept of being caught between two evils.

Chimera

The Chimera is a fearsome and monstrous creature with a hybrid body that combines the parts of multiple animals. Typically depicted as having the head and body of a lion, a goat's head emerging from its back, and a serpent or dragon as its tail, the Chimera is a symbol of chaos and destruction. The creature is also said to breathe fire, making it even more terrifying and formidable.

The Chimera plays a prominent role in the myth of Bellerophon, the hero who was tasked with slaying the beast. With the aid of the winged horse Pegasus, Bellerophon approached the Chimera from the air and successfully defeated it by driving a lead-tipped spear into its fiery throat, which melted and suffocated the creature. The Chimera's story represents the concept of overcoming seemingly insurmountable odds and the triumph of order over chaos. Its hybrid nature also makes it a powerful symbol of the unnatural and the monstrous, embodying the fears and challenges faced by ancient heroes.

Cyclopes

The Cyclopes are a race of giant beings known for their singular, enormous eye in the center of their forehead. There are two distinct groups of Cyclopes in myth. The first group, known as the Elder Cyclopes, are primordial beings and the offspring of Uranus (Sky) and Gaia (Earth). These Cyclopes, including Brontes, Steropes, and Arges, are skilled blacksmiths and craftsmen who forged Zeus's thunderbolts, Poseidon's trident, and Hades's helm of darkness. They played a crucial role in helping the Olympian gods overthrow the Titans.

The second group of Cyclopes, often associated with the Odyssey, are savage, solitary giants living in remote islands. The most famous of these is Polyphemus, who encounters Odysseus and his men. In Homer's Odyssey, Polyphemus captures Odysseus and his crew, intending to eat them, but Odysseus cunningly blinds the Cyclops and escapes. The Cyclopes in this context represent brute strength and primal power, often contrasted with the cleverness and resourcefulness of human heroes.

Cyclopes, whether as divine craftsmen or fearsome monsters, symbolize the raw, untamed forces of nature and the balance between creation and destruction in Greek mythology.

Empusa

Empusa is a fearsome female demon associated with the underworld and known for her ability to shapeshift. She is often depicted as a creature with one leg of bronze and the other of a donkey, giving her a grotesque and terrifying appearance. Empusa is a servant of the goddess Hecate, the goddess of witchcraft and the night, and is said to roam the earth at night, preying on young men and drinking their blood.

Empusa's role in mythology is primarily that of a nocturnal terror, embodying the fears associated with the night and the unknown. She is often mentioned in the context of stories meant to frighten and caution people against the dangers of wandering alone after dark. Empusa's ability to change her form adds to her menacing nature, as she can appear as a beautiful woman to lure her victims before revealing her true, horrifying form. Her presence in Greek mythology highlights the ancient Greeks' beliefs in supernatural creatures that lurk in the shadows, serving as a reminder of the dangers that exist beyond the safety of the familiar world.

Echidna

Echidna is a fearsome creature known as the "Mother of Monsters." She is often depicted as half-woman, half-serpent, with the upper body of a beautiful woman and the lower body of a fearsome snake. Echidna is the daughter of the primordial gods Phorcys and Ceto (or, in some versions, Tartarus and Gaia), and she is the mate of the monstrous giant Typhon. Together, Echidna and Typhon produced some of the most infamous monsters in Greek mythology, including the Hydra, Cerberus, the Chimera, the Sphinx, and the Nemean Lion.

Echidna's role in mythology is primarily as a progenitor of terror, giving birth to creatures that would become challenges for many of the greatest heroes, such as Heracles and Perseus. Although she herself does not play a prominent role in many myths, her offspring are central to numerous heroic tales, highlighting the constant battle between order and chaos. Echidna symbolizes the wild, untamed forces of nature and the dangers that lurk within the earth, making her a key figure in the mythological landscape of ancient Greece.

Furies (Erinyes)

The Furies, also known as the Erinyes, are ancient and powerful goddesses of vengeance and retribution. They are typically depicted as terrifying female figures with serpents entwined in their hair, blood dripping from their eyes, and wings of a bat or bird. The Furies are the daughters of Gaia (Earth) and the blood of Uranus (Sky), born from the drops of blood that fell when Uranus was castrated by his son Cronus.

The role of the Furies is to pursue and punish those who have committed heinous crimes, particularly those involving familial bloodshed, such as murder, perjury, and disrespect toward parents. They are relentless in their pursuit of justice, often driving their victims to madness or tormenting them until they repent or meet their fate. The Furies are not merely vengeful spirits but also enforcers of moral order, ensuring that the natural and divine laws are upheld.

The Furies are often invoked in Greek tragedies, such as Aeschylus's Oresteia, where they pursue Orestes for the murder of his mother, Clytemnestra. Their presence in Greek mythology represents the inescapable consequences of wrong-doing and the idea that justice, though harsh, is necessary to maintain balance in the world.

Gorgons

The Gorgons are three fearsome sisters known for their terrifying appearance and deadly gaze that could turn anyone who looked at them into stone. The most famous of the Gorgons is Medusa, the only mortal among them, while her sisters, Stheno and Euryale, are immortal. The Gorgons are often depicted with snakes for hair, bronze claws, and a hideous visage that strikes fear into the hearts of those who encounter them.

The Gorgons are the daughters of the sea deities Phorcys and Ceto, and they inhabit a desolate island far from the world of mortals. Medusa, the most well-known Gorgon, plays a central role in the myth of Perseus. Perseus, with the help of the gods, including Athena and Hermes, successfully beheads Medusa by using a mirrored shield to avoid her petrifying gaze. From Medusa's severed neck sprang the winged horse Pegasus and the giant Chrysaor.

The Gorgons symbolize the primal fear of the unknown and the monstrous, representing forces of chaos and destruction in the ancient world. Their story also highlights themes of beauty, transformation, and the power of the divine, as Medusa's head continues to wield its petrifying power even after her death, becoming a protective amulet known as the Gorgoneion.

Graeae

The Graeae are three ancient sisters who are the daughters of the sea deities Phorcys and Ceto. Their names are Deino, Enyo, and Pemphredo, and they are often referred to as the "Grey Sisters" or "Old Women" because they were born with gray hair and shared the appearance of old age from birth. The Graeae are unique in that they share a single eye and a single tooth among them, passing these between themselves as needed.

The Graeae play a crucial role in the myth of Perseus. To find and slay the Gorgon Medusa, Perseus sought out the Graeae to gain information about the location of the nymphs who possessed the magical items he needed for his quest, including the winged sandals, the kibisis (a special bag), and the cap of invisibility. By seizing their shared eye, Perseus forced the Graeae to reveal the information he needed before returning their eye and tooth.

The Graeae symbolize the mysterious and cryptic nature of ancient knowledge, as well as the idea of shared destiny and interdependence. Their portrayal as old and withered, yet still powerful and wise, reflects the reverence and fear of the ancient and the unknown in Greek mythology.

Griffin

The Griffin is a majestic and powerful creature with the body of a lion and the head and wings of an eagle. This hybrid symbolizes strength, courage, and vigilance, combining the king of beasts with the king of birds. Griffins are often depicted as guardians of treasures and sacred places, known for their fierce and protective nature.

Griffins are not tied to any specific myth but appear frequently in ancient art and literature as symbols of divine power and protection. They are often associated with guarding the gold deposits of the Scythians and other valuable treasures in remote regions, preventing theft by any who would seek to steal the riches. Griffins also embody the idea of balance, combining the earthly power of the lion with the celestial majesty of the eagle, and are sometimes seen as protectors of the divine and the natural order.

In Greek mythology and beyond, the Griffin represents the fusion of strength and intelligence, serving as a symbol of guardianship and the intersection between the earthly and the divine.

Harpies

Harpies are fearsome creatures with the body of a bird and the face of a woman. They are often depicted as winged women with sharp claws, known for their swiftness and ferocity. The name "Harpy" means "snatcher" or "swift robber," reflecting their role as agents of punishment who abduct and torment those who have angered the gods.

Harpies are most famously associated with the myth of Phineus, a blind prophet who was tormented by them as punishment for revealing too many divine secrets. The Harpies would snatch away or defile his food, leaving him in a constant state of hunger. They were eventually driven away by the Boreads, the winged sons of the North Wind, during the journey of the Argonauts.

In Greek mythology, Harpies symbolize the destructive forces of nature and the inescapable wrath of the gods. They are often seen as instruments of divine retribution, embodying the sudden, unpredictable nature of punishment and the relentless pursuit of those who have committed grave offenses.

Hecatoncheires

The Hecatoncheires are three gigantic beings known for their incredible strength and their hundred hands and fifty heads. Their name literally means "Hundred-Handed Ones." They are the offspring of the primordial deities Uranus (Sky) and Gaia (Earth) and are among the most powerful and fearsome creatures in Greek myth. The three Hecatoncheires are named Briareus (or Aegaeon), Cottus, and Gyges.

The role of the Hecatoncheires in mythology is pivotal during the Titanomachy, the great war between the Olympian gods, led by Zeus, and the Titans. Initially imprisoned by their father Uranus, and later by Cronus, they were freed by Zeus, who recognized their strength and sought their help in the battle against the Titans. In the war, the Hecatoncheires used their immense power to hurl massive boulders at the Titans, helping the Olympians secure victory.

The Hecatoncheires symbolize the overwhelming and chaotic forces of nature. Their loyalty to Zeus and their critical role in the defeat of the Titans highlight the theme of order triumphing over chaos in Greek mythology. After the war, they were given the role of guarding the imprisoned Titans in Tartarus, further emphasizing their association with strength and stability.

Hydra

The Hydra is a fearsome multi-headed serpent-like creature, known for its regenerative ability—when one of its heads is cut off, two more would grow in its place. The Hydra is the offspring of the monstrous giants Typhon and Echidna, making it part of a fearsome lineage of creatures. It dwells in the swamp of Lerna, near Argos, and its venom is so potent that even its breath is deadly.

The Hydra's most famous role is in the Twelve Labors of Heracles (Hercules), where it serves as the hero's second labor. To defeat the Hydra, Heracles, with the help of his nephew Iolaus, cauterized each neck with a torch immediately after severing a head, preventing new ones from growing. He eventually slayed the creature by crushing its immortal head under a boulder. After the battle, Heracles dipped his arrows in the Hydra's venomous blood, making them lethal weapons.

The Hydra symbolizes the idea of a seemingly insurmountable challenge, where efforts to resolve one problem lead to the emergence of new difficulties. Its defeat by Heracles represents the triumph of cunning and perseverance over overwhelming odds.

Lamia

Lamia is a tragic figure who transforms into a fearsome monster. She was originally a beautiful queen of Libya and a lover of Zeus, but when Hera, Zeus's jealous wife, discovered the affair, she exacted a cruel revenge by killing Lamia's children. Overcome with grief and madness, Lamia was transformed into a monstrous creature who preys on the children of others, often depicted as a serpentine or vampiric being.

Lamia's story embodies themes of loss, jealousy, and vengeance, as she becomes a symbol of maternal anguish turned into monstrous rage. In later myths, Lamia is portrayed as a night-dwelling creature who lures and devours children, feeding on their blood. Her legend served as a cautionary tale, particularly in ancient Greece, where she was often used to frighten children into good behavior.

Lamia's myth highlights the darker aspects of human emotions and the consequences of divine punishment. She represents the transformation of beauty and innocence into monstrosity, illustrating the destructive power of grief and the tragic consequences of divine wrath.

Manticore

The Manticore is a fearsome and legendary creature with the body of a lion, the head of a human, and a tail that is either a serpent or equipped with venomous spines, similar to that of a scorpion. Sometimes, it is also depicted with wings. The Manticore is said to have three rows of sharp teeth, and its name means "man-eater," reflecting its reputation as a deadly predator that devours humans whole, leaving no trace behind.

The Manticore originates from Persian mythology and was later adopted into Greek and Roman folklore. It is often portrayed as a monstrous creature that lurks in remote, dangerous places, preying on those who venture too close. The Manticore symbolizes the unknown and the terrifying forces of nature, blending different aspects of the animal kingdom into a single, formidable being. While not central to any specific myth, the Manticore embodies the fear of the wilderness and the monstrous, serving as a reminder of the dangers that lie beyond the boundaries of the known world.

Minotaur

The Minotaur is a monstrous creature with the body of a man and the head of a bull. He is the offspring of Pasiphaë, the wife of King Minos of Crete, and a majestic bull sent by the god Poseidon. The Minotaur was born as a result of a curse on Minos, who failed to sacrifice the bull to Poseidon as promised. Ashamed of the monstrous offspring, King Minos had the Minotaur imprisoned in the Labyrinth, an intricate maze designed by the master craftsman Daedalus, located beneath the palace of Knossos.

The Minotaur's role in mythology is most famously connected to the hero Theseus. As part of a punishment imposed by Minos, Athens was required to send seven young men and seven young women to Crete every nine years to be sacrificed to the Minotaur. Theseus volunteered to be one of the youths, with the intent to slay the beast and end the cycle of sacrifice. With the help of Minos's daughter, Ariadne, who gave him a ball of thread to navigate the Labyrinth, Theseus successfully found and killed the Minotaur, and then retraced his steps to escape the maze.

Nemean Lion

The Nemean Lion is a fearsome and invulnerable beast with golden fur that was impervious to weapons. It terrorized the region of Nemea, devouring livestock and people, and was known for its immense strength and invulnerability. The lion is most famous for being the target of the first of the Twelve Labors of Heracles (Hercules).

As part of his penance, Heracles was tasked with slaying the Nemean Lion. After realizing that his weapons were ineffective against the lion's tough hide, Heracles used his immense strength to wrestle the beast and ultimately kill it by strangling it with his bare hands. Afterward, Heracles skinned the lion using its own claws, and he wore the lion's impenetrable hide as armor, which became one of his most iconic attributes.

Nymphs

Nymphs are divine spirits and minor goddesses associated with various aspects of nature. They are often depicted as beautiful, youthful maidens who inhabit and personify natural features such as rivers, forests, mountains, and groves. Nymphs are generally benevolent beings who embody the life-giving and nurturing aspects of nature, but they can also be mischievous and elusive.

There are several different types of nymphs, each linked to a specific element of the natural world. For example, Dryads are nymphs of the trees, particularly oak trees; Naiads are freshwater nymphs associated with rivers, springs, and lakes; Oreads are mountain nymphs; and Oceanids are sea nymphs, daughters of the Titan Oceanus. Nymphs often play roles in various myths, interacting with gods and mortals alike, sometimes offering help or companionship, and other times becoming the objects of pursuit in romantic tales.

Pegasus

Pegasus is a magnificent winged horse born from the blood of the Gorgon Medusa after she was slain by the hero Perseus. According to myth, when Perseus beheaded Medusa, Pegasus and his brother Chrysaor sprang forth from her neck, both being the offspring of Medusa and the god Poseidon. Pegasus is known for his pure white color and his ability to fly, making him one of the most iconic and beloved creatures in Greek mythology.

Pegasus plays a key role in the myth of Bellerophon, a hero who tamed Pegasus with the help of a golden bridle given to him by the goddess Athena. Together, Bellerophon and Pegasus embarked on several heroic adventures, the most famous being the defeat of the Chimera, a fire-breathing monster. After completing his heroic deeds, Pegasus ascended to the heavens, where he was transformed into a constellation by Zeus, immortalizing his place in the night sky.

Satyrs

Satyrs are mischievous and lustful woodland creatures who are often depicted with the upper body of a man and the lower body of a goat, including goat-like ears, legs, and horns. They are closely associated with Dionysus, the god of wine, revelry, and ecstasy, and they embody the untamed and hedonistic aspects of nature. Satyrs are known for their love of music, dancing, drinking, and pursuing nymphs, often participating in the wild, ecstatic rites of Dionysian worship.

Satyrs are typically portrayed as companions of Dionysus, joining him in his bacchanalian processions and celebrating the pleasures of life without restraint. In myths and art, they are often depicted playing musical instruments like the panpipes or lyres, engaging in dance, or chasing after nymphs in pursuit of their desires. Satyrs represent the primal, instinctual side of humanity, free from societal constraints, and are a symbol of the natural world's wild, chaotic energy.

Scylla

Scylla is a terrifying sea monster who resides on one side of a narrow strait, opposite the whirlpool Charybdis. Once a beautiful nymph, Scylla was transformed into a monstrous creature by the sorceress Circe, who was jealous of Scylla's beauty. Scylla's body became surrounded by multiple vicious dog-like heads and twelve tentacle-like legs, each head snapping at anything that came too close. Her lower body is often depicted as a cluster of writhing serpents or tentacles.

Scylla's role in mythology is most famously detailed in Homer's Odyssey. As Odysseus and his crew navigate the dangerous strait between Scylla and Charybdis, they must choose which peril to face. Odysseus opts to sail closer to Scylla, sacrificing a few of his men to her snapping jaws rather than risking the entire ship being swallowed by Charybdis's whirlpool. Scylla thus represents the unavoidable dangers and difficult choices that often confront heroes on their journeys.

Sirens

The Sirens are enchanting creatures known for their irresistible and mesmerizing singing voices that lured sailors to their doom. They are often depicted as half-woman, half-bird, with the upper body of a beautiful woman and the lower body of a bird, though later representations sometimes portray them as mermaid-like figures. The Sirens lived on rocky islands or cliffs, and their songs were so alluring that mariners who heard them would steer their ships toward the sound, only to crash on the treacherous rocks and perish.

The most famous encounter with the Sirens occurs in Homer's Odyssey, where the hero Odysseus must navigate past them on his journey home. Forewarned of the danger, Odysseus orders his men to plug their ears with beeswax and has himself tied to the mast of his ship so that he can safely hear their song without succumbing to its deadly allure. This episode highlights the themes of temptation, self-control, and the perils of giving in to desire.

Sphinx

The Sphinx is a mysterious and formidable creature with the body of a lion, the wings of an eagle, and the head of a woman. She is most famously associated with the myth of Oedipus and is known for her role as a guardian of the city of Thebes. The Sphinx posed a deadly riddle to all who attempted to pass her: "What walks on four legs in the morning, two legs at noon, and three legs in the evening?" Those who could not answer correctly were devoured by the Sphinx.

Oedipus, on his journey to Thebes, encountered the Sphinx and successfully answered her riddle: "Man, who crawls on all fours as a baby, walks on two legs as an adult, and uses a cane in old age." With the riddle solved, the Sphinx was defeated and, in some versions of the myth, threw herself off a cliff in despair. This victory allowed Oedipus to continue on to Thebes, where he would later become king, setting the stage for the tragic events of his life.

Stymphalian Birds

The Stymphalian Birds are a flock of monstrous, man-eating birds with metallic feathers that they could launch like deadly arrows. These fearsome creatures were said to inhabit the marshes around Lake Stymphalus in Arcadia. They were a scourge to the region, attacking crops, livestock, and even humans with their sharp, bronze-like beaks and poisonous droppings.

The Stymphalian Birds play a key role in the myth of Heracles (Hercules), where they are featured as the sixth of his Twelve Labors. Heracles was tasked with driving these dangerous birds away from the Stymphalian marshes. To accomplish this, he used a set of bronze castanets given to him by the goddess Athena to create a loud, clattering noise that frightened the birds into the air. As they took flight, Heracles shot many of them down with his bow and arrows, and the remainder fled, never to return.

Talos

Talos is a giant bronze automaton created by the god Hephaestus, or in some versions, by the inventor Daedalus. He was designed to protect the island of Crete from invaders and was gifted to King Minos. Talos was a living, animated statue made entirely of bronze, with veins of molten metal running through his body. He patrolled the shores of Crete, circling the island three times a day and hurling rocks at approaching ships to keep enemies at bay.

Talos's role in mythology is as a guardian and protector, embodying the concept of an unyielding, mechanical sentinel. His one vulnerability was a single vein sealed by a bronze nail, which, when removed, would cause him to lose his life force. Talos met his end when the Argonauts, on their quest for the Golden Fleece, encountered him. According to one version of the myth, Medea, the sorceress accompanying the Argonauts, used her magic to remove the nail or tricked Talos into doing it himself, causing the life-giving ichor to flow out and ultimately leading to his death.

Talos represents the fusion of technology and mythology, symbolizing the ancient Greeks' exploration of artificial life and the limits of human craftsmanship. His story highlights the themes of protection, vulnerability, and the intersection of human ingenuity with the natural world.

Typhon

Typhon, in Greek mythology, is one of the most fearsome and powerful monsters, often described as the "father of all monsters." He is the son of Gaia (Earth) and Tartarus (the deep abyss), and his appearance is terrifying: Typhon is depicted as a giant with a hundred dragon heads, each spewing fire, and his lower body is made up of massive coils of serpents. His wings could blot out the sun, and his voice was said to be a mix of all animal sounds.

Typhon's role in mythology is primarily as the greatest adversary of the Olympian gods. After the Titans were defeated by the Olympians, Gaia, angry at the loss of her children, gave birth to Typhon to challenge Zeus's rule. In the ensuing battle, known as the Typhonomachy, Typhon initially overwhelmed the gods, forcing them to flee. However, Zeus eventually confronted Typhon and, after a fierce struggle, defeated him by hurling thunderbolts, trapping Typhon beneath Mount Etna in Sicily, where his writhing is said to cause volcanic eruptions.

Typhon symbolizes the chaotic and destructive forces of nature, representing the ultimate challenge to divine order and authority. His defeat by Zeus solidifies the Olympian gods' control over the cosmos, marking the triumph of order over chaos. Typhon's story highlights the themes of power, rebellion, and the eternal struggle between opposing forces in the universe.

CHAPTER 4: LIFE IN ANCIENT GREECE

Ancient Greece, known for its remarkable contributions to art, philosophy, politics, and science, was a civilization that flourished from the archaic period in the 8th century BCE to the end of antiquity around 600 CE. It was a collection of city-states, or poleis, the most famous being Athens, Sparta, Corinth, and Thebes. Each city-state had its own government, laws, and customs, but they shared a common language, religion, and cultural heritage.

Greek society was stratified, with a clear hierarchy that included free citizens, women, children, slaves, and foreigners. Citizens had political rights and responsibilities, while women and slaves were often excluded from political life. Despite these social distinctions, the Greeks were united by their belief in the pantheon of gods and goddesses who played a central role in their daily lives and cultural practices.

Daily Life in Ancient Greece

Daily life in ancient Greece varied significantly based on social status, gender, and location, but it was primarily centered around the household, or oikos. The household included not just the nuclear family but also extended relatives and slaves, forming the basic unit of society.

For men, daily life involved various activities outside the home. They engaged in public life, participating in politics, commerce, and military endeavors. The agora, or marketplace, was a central hub where men gathered to discuss politics, philosophy, and current events. It was a place of social interaction and economic activity, bustling with merchants, craftsmen, and buyers. Men also spent time in the gymnasium, where they engaged in physical exercise, trained for athletic competitions, and socialized. Education was a crucial aspect of a young man's life, with boys being trained in a range of subjects including literature, music, and physical education. This education prepared them for active participation in civic l ife.

Women, on the other hand, led more confined lives within the home. Their primary responsibilities included managing the household, supervising slaves, and raising children. Women were expected to ensure the smooth running of domestic affairs, from food preparation to weaving and other household crafts. They had limited rights and their activities were largely restricted to the private sphere. However, some women did play important roles in religious activities and festivals, participating in ceremonies and serving as priestesses. Despite their limited public roles, women's contributions to the household were vital to the overall functioning of Greek society.

Children's lives were also defined by their gender. Boys were educated from a young age in various disciplines, including reading, writing, music, and physical training. Their education was designed to prepare them for future roles as active citizens and soldiers. Girls, on the other hand, received their education at home, learning domestic skills from their mothers. They were trained to manage the household and fulfill their roles as wives and mothers in the future.

Slaves were an integral part of Greek society and were involved in a wide range of activities. They performed household chores, worked in the fields, and assisted in various trades and crafts. Slaves were considered property and had very few rights, though their treatment varied depending on their masters and the nature of their work. Some slaves could earn their freedom, but many lived their entire lives in servitude.

Daily routines in ancient Greece were also marked by a strong sense of community and religious observance. Meals were typically simple, consisting of bread, olives, cheese, fruits, and occasionally meat or fish. Social gatherings and symposia were common, where men would come together to drink, converse, and enjoy entertainment.

How the Greeks Worshipped Their Gods

The Greeks worshipped their gods through a rich tapestry of rituals, ceremonies, and daily practices that permeated every aspect of their lives. Religion was not confined to a specific day or place but was an integral part of their everyday existence, influencing their homes, public spaces, and community activities.

In the household, worship centered around the hearth, which was considered sacred to Hestia, the goddess of hearth and home. Each day, families would make small offerings to Hestia to ensure her protection and favor. These offerings often included food, wine, and incense. Additionally, households would honor other domestic deities and spirits, such as the household gods known as Lares and Penates, who were believed to protect the home and family.

Public worship was an important aspect of Greek religious life and was conducted in temples, open-air altars, and communal spaces. Each city-state had its patron deity, and the most prominent temples were dedicated to these gods. For instance, Athens honored Athena with the Parthenon, while Olympia revered Zeus with a grand temple. Public worship involved elaborate rituals conducted by priests and priestesses, who were often selected from noble families. These rituals included prayers, hymns, and the presentation of offerings, such as food, wine, and valuable items.

Animal sacrifices were a central component of Greek worship and were performed to gain the favor of the gods. These sacrifices were elaborate ceremonies
that involved the slaughtering of animals, typically bulls, goats, or sheep, on
altars outside the temples. The animals were often adorned with garlands and
purified with water before being sacrificed. The meat was then divided, with
portions burned for the gods and the rest distributed among the worshippers for a
communal feast. This practice not only served as a religious act but also reinforced
social bonds within the community.

Festivals were another significant element of Greek religious practice, providing
opportunities for collective worship and celebration. These festivals varied in scale
and purpose, often including athletic competitions, music, dance, theatrical performances, and processions. One of the most famous festivals was the Olympic
Games, held every four years in Olympia to honor Zeus. Athletes from across
Greece competed in various sports, and the event fostered a sense of unity and
shared identity among the Greek city-states.

Another major festival was the Panathenaic Festival in Athens, dedicated to
Athena. This festival featured a grand procession to the Acropolis, where a new
robe (peplos) was presented to the statue of Athena. The procession included
citizens of all ages and statuses, and the event culminated in sacrifices and feasting.
The Dionysia, held in honor of Dionysus, was notable for its dramatic competitions, which laid the foundation for Greek theater. During this festival, playwrights presented their works in a contest, and the performances were attended
by large audiences.

Mystery religions and cults also played a role in Greek worship, offering more
personal and esoteric religious experiences. The Eleusinian Mysteries, dedicated
to Demeter and Persephone, were among the most famous. Initiates underwent
secret rites that promised them a blessed afterlife. These mysteries were highly
secretive, and the details of the rituals were closely guarded.

Oracles and divination were another crucial aspect of Greek religious life. The most famous oracle was the Oracle of Delphi, where the priestess Pythia, believed to be inspired by Apollo, delivered prophecies. Individuals and city-states consulted the oracle for guidance on important matters, from personal decisions to state affairs. The process involved offering sacrifices and gifts to the god, after which the priestess would enter a trance and deliver enigmatic messages that required interpretation.

In addition to these formal practices, the Greeks also engaged in spontaneous acts of devotion, such as praying at roadside shrines, making votive offerings at sacred springs, and dedicating small statues or inscriptions to the gods. These acts reflected the pervasive presence of the divine in their lives and their belief in the gods' active involvement in the world.

Temples, Rituals, and Festivals

Temples, rituals, and festivals were central to the religious life of ancient Greece, providing structured ways for individuals and communities to honor the gods and ensure their favor. Temples were monumental structures, often built in prominent locations within city-states, serving as both religious centers and symbols of civic pride. These edifices were not just places of worship but were considered the earthly homes of the gods. Inside the temples, magnificent statues of the deities, crafted from materials like marble and gold, were housed in the inner sanctum, or cella. These statues were more than artistic representations; they were believed to embody the divine presence, making the temple a sacred space.

The construction of a temple was a community effort, often funded by the city-state and involving the finest architects and artists. The architecture itself was designed to reflect the glory of the gods, with columns, friezes, and pediments adorned with intricate carvings depicting mythological scenes. These structures were both awe-inspiring and functional, facilitating various religious activities.

Rituals performed at these temples were elaborate and meticulously planned, reflecting the importance of precise execution to avoid offending the gods. One of the most significant rituals was animal sacrifice, which involved a series of steps to ensure the ritual's sanctity. The animal, often a bull, sheep, or goat, was chosen based on its perceived purity and suitability as an offering. Before the sacrifice, the animal was adorned with garlands and purified with water, symbolizing its readiness to be offered to the gods. The actual sacrifice was a solemn event, often accompanied by prayers and hymns, where the animal was slaughtered, and its blood was collected and poured over the altar. Parts of the animal were then burned as an offering to the deity, while the remaining meat was cooked and shared in a communal feast, reinforcing social bonds and communal identity.

Libations and votive offerings were also integral parts of Greek worship. Libations, or the pouring of liquids such as wine, oil, or honey, were common rituals performed to honor the gods and seek their blessings. These offerings were poured onto the ground, altars, or special vessels, symbolizing the act of giving back to the gods. Votive offerings, including statues, jewelry, and other valuable items, were dedicated to the gods as acts of gratitude or supplication. These offerings were often inscribed with the donor's name and the purpose of the dedication, serving as tangible tokens of devotion.

Festivals were vibrant, multifaceted events that brought together communities to celebrate and honor the gods. These festivals were held regularly throughout the year and were significant both religiously and socially. They provided opportunities for communal worship, entertainment, and the reinforcement of social cohesion. The Olympic Games, dedicated to Zeus, were one of the most renowned festivals, drawing participants and spectators from across the Greek world. These games included athletic competitions such as running, wrestling, and chariot racing, with victors gaining honor and prestige not only for themselves but also for their city-states.

The Panathenaic Festival in Athens, dedicated to Athena, was another major event. This festival featured a grand procession through the city, culminating at the Acropolis, where a new robe was presented to the statue of Athena. The festival included athletic contests, musical performances, and dramatic presentations, making it a major cultural and religious occasion. The Dionysia, dedicated to Dionysus, was notable for its dramatic competitions, which laid the foundation for Greek theater. Playwrights like Aeschylus, Sophocles, and Euripides presented their works, exploring complex themes and human experiences, with the performances attended by large, engaged audiences.

In addition to these major festivals, numerous local festivals were held throughout the year, each with its own unique rituals and customs. These festivals often involved processions, sacrifices, feasts, and various forms of entertainment, reflecting the rich diversity of Greek religious practice. Mystery religions, such as the Eleusinian Mysteries dedicated to Demeter and Persephone, offered more personal and esoteric religious experiences. Initiates underwent secret rites that promised them a blessed afterlife, fostering a deep sense of spiritual fulfillment and community among participants.

Overall, the temples, rituals, and festivals of ancient Greece were more than just religious activities; they were integral to the social and cultural fabric of Greek life. These practices provided structured means to worship, celebrate, and communicate with the gods, reinforcing social cohesion and cultural values. Through their elaborate rituals and grand festivals, the Greeks expressed their reverence, sought divine guidance, and celebrated their mythological heritage, creating a lasting legacy that continues to captivate and inspire.

CHAPTER 5: THE GREEK CREATION MYTH

The Greek creation myth is a fascinating tale that describes the origins of the universe and the lineage of gods and goddesses who govern the world. It is a story filled with dramatic events, powerful deities, and cosmic battles, reflecting the ancient Greeks' attempt to explain the nature of existence and the forces that shape their world.

The myth begins with Chaos, the formless void from which everything emerged. Chaos was not a deity in the traditional sense but rather a primordial state of disorder and emptiness. From Chaos, the first primordial deities arose, embodying fundamental aspects of the universe. These deities included Gaia (Earth), Tartarus (the abyss), Eros (love), Erebus (darkness), and Nyx (night).

Gaia, the personification of Earth, soon gave birth to Uranus (the sky) and Pontus (the sea). Gaia and Uranus became the first divine couple, and their union produced the first generation of powerful beings known as the Titans. The Titans included Cronus, Rhea, Oceanus, Tethys, Hyperion, Theia, Coeus, Phoebe, Crius, Mnemosyne, Themis, and Iapetus. These Titans represented various aspects of the natural world and human experience.

However, the relationship between Gaia and Uranus was troubled. Uranus, fearing the power of his offspring, imprisoned some of them, including the Cyclopes and the Hecatoncheires (hundred-handed giants), deep within Gaia. Anguished by her children's suffering, Gaia conspired with her youngest Titan son, Cronus, to overthrow Uranus. Cronus ambushed Uranus, castrated him with a sickle, and took his place as the ruler of the cosmos. From the blood of Uranus, several other beings were born, including the Furies, the Giants, and the Meliae (ash tree nymphs).

Cronus's rule, known as the Golden Age, was marked by prosperity and abundance. However, Cronus was also warned by a prophecy that he would be overthrown by one of his own children, just as he had overthrown Uranus. To prevent this, Cronus swallowed each of his offspring at birth. His wife, Rhea, distraught at the loss of her children, devised a plan to save her youngest son, Zeus. When Zeus was born, Rhea hid him in a cave on the island of Crete and gave Cronus a stone wrapped in swaddling clothes, which he swallowed, believing it to be his son.

Zeus grew up in secret and, upon reaching adulthood, sought to challenge his father. With the help of Metis, a Titaness, Zeus tricked Cronus into drinking a potion that caused him to vomit up his swallowed children: Hestia, Demeter, Hera, Hades, and Poseidon. United, Zeus and his siblings declared war on Cronus and the other Titans, leading to the great cosmic battle known as the Titanomachy (this is covered in more detail in Chapter 6).

The Titanomachy was a protracted and brutal conflict that lasted for ten years. Zeus and his siblings, aided by the Cyclopes (who forged Zeus's thunderbolts) and the Hecatoncheires, ultimately triumphed over the Titans. The defeated Titans were imprisoned in Tartarus, a deep abyss, guarded by the Hecatoncheires. However, some Titans, such as Prometheus and Epimetheus, who sided with Zeus, were spared this fate.

With the Titans defeated, Zeus and his siblings established a new order, becoming the Olympian gods. Zeus took his place as the king of the gods, ruling from Mount Olympus. His brothers and sisters were given dominion over various aspects of the world: Poseidon became the god of the sea, Hades the ruler of the

Underworld, Hera the goddess of marriage and family, Demeter the goddess of the harvest, and Hestia the goddess of the hearth and home.

The rise of Zeus and the Olympians marked the beginning of a new era in Greek mythology. Under their rule, the world was populated with humans and other creatures, and the gods interacted frequently with mortals, shaping their destinies and influencing the course of history. The Olympians became central figures in countless myths and legends, embodying the Greeks' understanding of the divine and its relationship with the mortal world.

Variations of the Greek creation myth exist, with different sources offering slightly different accounts of the events and characters involved. However, the core themes of chaos giving rise to order, the succession of divine rulers, and the interplay of power and prophecy remain consistent, reflecting the ancient Greeks' view of a dynamic and ever-changing cosmos governed by powerful, often capricious deities.

CHAPTER 6: THE TITANOMACHY

The Titanomachy, a colossal war between the Titans and the Olympians, stands as one of the most dramatic and defining conflicts in Greek mythology. This epic battle, which spanned ten years, ultimately led to the overthrow of the Titans and the rise of the Olympian gods, reshaping the divine hierarchy of the ancient world.

The seeds of the Titanomachy were sown in the early days of creation, following the rise of the Titans under the leadership of Cronus. After dethroning his father Uranus, Cronus assumed control of the cosmos. His reign, though initially marked by prosperity, was shadowed by a prophecy foretelling his eventual overthrow by one of his own offspring. In a desperate attempt to prevent this fate, Cronus swallowed each of his children immediately after birth, ensuring they could not grow up to challenge him.

Rhea, Cronus's wife and sister, was devastated by the loss of her children. Determined to save her youngest son, Zeus, she devised a plan. When Zeus was born, Rhea hid him in a cave on the island of Crete, entrusting him to the care of the nymphs Adrasteia and Ida, and the goat Amalthea. To deceive Cronus, Rhea swaddled a stone in cloth and presented it to him as their newborn child. Unaware of the ruse, Cronus swallowed the stone, believing he had thwarted the prophecy once more.

Zeus grew up in secrecy, nurtured by the nymphs and Amalthea. As he matured, he became increasingly aware of his destiny and the need to rescue his siblings and challenge Cronus's tyrannical rule. With wisdom and strength on his side, Zeus sought the counsel of Metis, a Titaness known for her wisdom and cunning. Together, they concocted a plan to free his siblings and begin the rebellion against Cronus.

Disguised as a cupbearer, Zeus infiltrated Cronus's court and administered a potion, crafted by Metis, into Cronus's drink. The potion caused Cronus to regurgitate the stone he had swallowed, followed by Zeus's siblings: Hestia, Demeter, Hera, Hades, and Poseidon. Reunited, the liberated gods pledged their loyalty to Zeus and prepared for the impending conflict.

The Titanomachy began in earnest as Zeus and his siblings declared war on Cronus and the Titans. The battle lines were drawn, with the Titans, led by Cronus, occupying Mount Othrys, and the Olympians, led by Zeus, fortifying themselves on Mount Olympus. The conflict quickly escalated into a fierce and protracted war, with both sides wielding immense power and seeking allies to bolster their ranks.

Zeus sought the support of the Cyclopes and the Hecatoncheires, who had been imprisoned by Cronus deep within Tartarus. The Cyclopes, grateful for their liberation, bestowed powerful gifts upon Zeus and his siblings: thunderbolts for Zeus, a trident for Poseidon, and a helmet of invisibility for Hades. These formidable weapons significantly enhanced the Olympians' combat abilities. The Hecatoncheires, with their hundred hands and immense strength, also joined the Olympian cause, providing crucial reinforcement.

The war raged on, marked by a series of intense and cataclysmic battles. The earth shook and the heavens trembled as the Titans and Olympians clashed. Mount Othrys and Mount Olympus became battlegrounds where the fate of the cosmos hung in the balance. The Titans, powerful and experienced, fought with all their might, but the Olympians, driven by their desire for justice and liberation, matched their ferocity.

One of the key moments in the war was the betrayal of the Titan Prometheus. Foreseeing the eventual victory of the Olympians, Prometheus chose to side with Zeus, providing valuable strategic counsel and aiding in the capture of critical strongholds. His defection weakened the Titans' position and bolstered the Olympian resolve.

The final, decisive battle saw the full might of the Olympians unleashed. Zeus, wielding his thunderbolts, led the charge, while Poseidon and Hades used their trident and helmet of invisibility to great effect. The Hecatoncheires hurled massive boulders, creating chaos among the Titans. The sheer force and determination of the Olympians eventually overwhelmed the Titans, culminating in the defeat of Cronus and his allies.

With the Titans vanquished, Zeus and his siblings established a new divine order. The defeated Titans were imprisoned in the depths of Tartarus, guarded by the Hecatoncheires, ensuring they could not rise again to challenge the Olympians. Cronus's reign was over, and the age of the Olympian gods began.

Zeus assumed his role as the king of the gods, ruling from Mount Olympus alongside his siblings. Each god and goddess was assigned dominion over specific aspects of the world: Zeus as the god of the sky and thunder, Poseidon as the god of the sea, Hades as the ruler of the Underworld, Hera as the goddess of marriage and family, Demeter as the goddess of the harvest, and Hestia as the goddess of the hearth and home.

The Titanomachy not only established the Olympians as the new rulers of the cosmos but also set the stage for many of the myths and legends that followed. It symbolized the triumph of a new order over the old, the victory of justice and liberation over tyranny and oppression. The epic struggle between the Titans and the Olympians remains a cornerstone of Greek mythology, illustrating the timeless themes of power, rebellion, and the quest for supremacy.

CHAPTER 7: THE MYTH OF PROMETHEUS

The myth of Prometheus is one of the most profound and enduring stories in Greek mythology, embodying themes of defiance, punishment, and the quest for knowledge. Prometheus, a Titan known for his wisdom and foresight, played a pivotal role in the creation and development of humanity, often challenging the will of Zeus and the other Olympian gods. His tale is rich with complexity and has been interpreted in various ways throughout history.

Prometheus was one of the second-generation Titans, the son of Iapetus and Clymene. Unlike many of his fellow Titans, who were embroiled in the struggle against the Olympians during the Titanomachy, Prometheus chose to side with Zeus, foreseeing the ultimate victory of the Olympian gods. This decision initially earned him a place of respect among the new rulers of the cosmos.

One of the most significant contributions of Prometheus to Greek mythology is his role in the creation of humanity. According to some versions of the myth, Prometheus and his brother Epimetheus were tasked by the gods with creating all living creatures. Epimetheus, whose name means "afterthought," hastily distributed various gifts and abilities to the animals, such as speed, strength, and camouflage. By the time he reached humanity, he had run out of gifts. Seeing humanity's vulnerability, Prometheus, whose name means "forethought," took it upon himself to give humans the qualities that would enable them to survive and thrive.

Prometheus shaped humans out of clay, infusing them with life. However, he soon realized that his creations were defenseless against the elements and the dangers of the world. To rectify this, Prometheus decided to bestow upon humanity the gift of fire, an element that was strictly reserved for the gods. Fire represented knowledge, technology, and the ability to progress and evolve. Prometheus knew that stealing fire from the gods was a grave act of defiance, but he believed that humanity's potential justified the risk.

In a daring act, Prometheus ascended to Olympus and stole fire from the forge of Hephaestus, hiding it in a hollow fennel stalk. He then brought the fire down to earth and gave it to humanity. With fire, humans could cook food, keep warm, craft tools, and develop civilization. This gift marked a turning point in human history, allowing people to rise above their primal state and begin building societies.

Zeus, however, was enraged by Prometheus's audacity. He viewed the theft of fire as a direct challenge to his authority and an affront to the divine order. To punish Prometheus and humanity, Zeus devised a series of retaliatory actions. First, he ordered the creation of Pandora, the first woman, who was fashioned by Hephaestus and endowed with beauty and charm by the other gods. Pandora was given a jar (often mistakenly referred to as a box) containing all the evils of the world. She was sent to Epimetheus, who, despite Prometheus's warnings, accepted her as his wife. Driven by curiosity, Pandora eventually opened the jar, releasing plagues, sorrows, and misfortunes upon humanity, leaving only hope inside.

Zeus's vengeance did not end with Pandora. He reserved a particularly harsh punishment for Prometheus. The Titan was seized by Zeus's minions, Force and Violence, and taken to the remote mountains of the Caucasus. There, Prometheus was chained to a rock with unbreakable bonds crafted by Hephaestus. As part of his eternal torment, Zeus sent an eagle, a symbol of his power, to tear at Prometheus's liver every day. Being immortal, Prometheus's liver would regenerate each night, only for the eagle to return and devour it again the next day. This cycle of suffering was intended to last for eternity, serving as a stark warning to any who might dare defy the king of the gods.

Despite his unbearable agony, Prometheus remained defiant and unyielding. His suffering garnered the sympathy of many, including mortals and some gods. Over time, the myth of Prometheus evolved to include various versions of his eventual release. One of the most popular accounts involves the hero Heracles, a son of Zeus known for his extraordinary strength and valor. During his Twelve Labors, Heracles passed through the Caucasus Mountains and came across Prometheus in his tortured state. Moved by his plight, Heracles killed the eagle and broke Prometheus's chains, freeing the Titan from his torment. This act of compassion and heroism was tolerated by Zeus, possibly because Heracles was his son and because Prometheus had already endured considerable punishment.

Prometheus's story did not end with his release. According to some myths, he continued to play a role in the affairs of gods and men. He retained his reputation as a protector of humanity and a symbol of resistance against tyranny. The myth of Prometheus also inspired numerous interpretations and retellings in literature, philosophy, and art, from the works of Aeschylus, who wrote the tragic play "Prometheus Bound," to the Romantic poets who saw in Prometheus a figure of noble defiance and suffering for the sake of humanity.

CHAPTER 8: THE 12 LABORS OF HERACLES

Heracles, known to the Romans as Hercules, is one of the most celebrated heroes in Greek mythology. Renowned for his incredible strength and bravery, Heracles was the son of Zeus, the king of the gods, and Alcmene, a mortal woman. This divine heritage granted him extraordinary abilities, but it also subjected him to intense scrutiny and hostility, particularly from Hera, Zeus's wife. Hera's animosity towards Heracles stemmed from her jealousy and resentment of Zeus's infidelities. As the illegitimate child of her unfaithful husband, Heracles became the target of Hera's wrath.

From the moment of his birth, Hera sought to destroy Heracles. She sent two serpents to kill him in his crib, but the infant Heracles, already displaying his prodigious strength, strangled the snakes with his bare hands. This early demonstration of his divine power only intensified Hera's desire to see him suffer. Throughout his life, Hera's interference caused numerous hardships for Heracles, but none were as severe as the madness she inflicted upon him.

In a fit of divine-induced insanity, Hera caused Heracles to kill his wife, Megara, and their children. When he regained his sanity and realized the horrors he had committed, he was devastated and sought purification for his actions. To atone for his sins, the Oracle of Delphi instructed him to serve King Eurystheus of Tiryns for twelve years. Eurystheus, taking advantage of this opportunity and influenced by Hera, assigned Heracles twelve seemingly impossible labors, hoping to rid himself of the hero. Each labor tested Heracles's strength, courage, and ingenuity, forging his legacy as one of the greatest heroes in Greek mythology.

The First Labor: The Nemean Lion

Heracles's first labor, assigned by King Eurystheus, was to slay the Nemean Lion, a monstrous beast terrorizing the region of Nemea. This task was deliberately chosen by Eurystheus, influenced by Hera, who sought to humiliate and, ideally, destroy Heracles through these impossible labors. The Nemean Lion was no ordinary creature; it was a formidable beast with a hide that was impervious to any weapon, making it invulnerable to conventional attacks. This lion had been wreaking havoc in the area, killing livestock, and threatening the inhabitants of Nemea, who lived in constant fear of its attacks.

Heracles set out on his journey to Nemea, determined to prove his worth and complete the task. Upon arriving in the region, he began his search for the lion. The local villagers, terrified and weary from the constant threat, provided Heracles with little information, as many had never seen the beast and only heard its terrifying roars from a distance. Heracles scouted the area for days, tracking the lion through the dense forests and rocky terrain. He examined the carcasses of animals left in the lion's wake, studying the beast's patterns and movements.

Once evening, as Heracles was resting near a stream, he heard the distant roar of the lion. He quickly armed himself with his bow and a quiver of arrows, his sword, and a club he had fashioned from an olive tree. Following the sound, he soon came upon the lion's tracks and followed them to the entrance of a cave. The cave had two openings, which the lion used to move in and out freely. Heracles decided to confront the lion within its lair, where the confined space would prevent the beast from escaping or launching surprise attacks.

As he approached the cave, Heracles prepared his bow and aimed an arrow at the lion, which was resting near the entrance. He released the arrow with great force, but to his astonishment, it simply bounced off the lion's impenetrable hide. The lion, enraged by the attack, sprang to its feet and charged at Heracles with incredible speed and ferocity. Heracles quickly drew his sword and struck at the beast, but the blade shattered upon contact with the lion's invulnerable fur. Realizing that conventional weapons were useless, Heracles retreated deeper into the cave, luring the lion into the narrow confines of the cavern.

Inside the cave, Heracles used his immense strength and agility to his advantage. He picked up his club and swung it at the lion with all his might, aiming for its head. The lion was stunned but not seriously harmed, as its thick skull absorbed much of the impact. Heracles knew he had to change his tactics. He dropped the club and decided to engage the lion in close combat, relying on his strength and wrestling skills.

The battle between Heracles and the Nemean Lion was intense and brutal. Heracles grappled with the beast, using his powerful arms to avoid its deadly claws and teeth. The lion, in turn, fought fiercely, trying to overpower the hero. After a grueling struggle, Heracles managed to wrap his arms around the lion's neck, applying a vice-like grip. He squeezed with all his might, using his immense strength to choke the life out of the beast. The lion thrashed and roared in desperation, but Heracles's grip was unrelenting. Eventually, the lion's struggles weakened, and it collapsed to the ground, dead.

Exhausted but victorious, Heracles stood over the lifeless body of the Nemean Lion. He had succeeded in completing his first labor, but his task was not yet over. As proof of his triumph, Heracles needed to skin the lion and bring its pelt back to King Eurystheus. However, the lion's impenetrable hide posed a new challenge. Heracles attempted to use his knife to cut through the fur but quickly realized that no blade could pierce it. He then remembered the lion's own claws, which were sharp and strong enough to penetrate its hide. Using one of the lion's claws, Heracles carefully skinned the beast, removing the pelt intact.

Heracles donned the lion's pelt as a cloak, which provided him with protection and symbolized his victory. The lion's head, worn as a hood, gave him a fearsome appearance, and the pelt itself was invulnerable, much like the beast it once covered. Wearing the pelt, Heracles returned to Tiryns to present his trophy to Eurystheus. Upon seeing Heracles and the lion's pelt, Eurystheus was both astonished and terrified. He had underestimated Heracles's strength and resourcefulness.

To ensure his own safety, Eurystheus forbade Heracles from entering the city. Instead, he ordered the hero to present the results of his labors from outside the city gates. Furthermore, Eurystheus commissioned a large bronze jar, which he used as a hiding place whenever Heracles approached, showcasing his cowardice and fear of the mighty hero.

The Second Labor: The Lernaean Hydra

For his second labor, King Eurystheus assigned Heracles the daunting task of slaying the Lernaean Hydra, a fearsome serpent-like monster with multiple heads that terrorized the region of Lerna. This labor, like the first, was influenced by Hera, who hoped that Heracles would meet his end battling the seemingly invincible creature. The Hydra was said to have nine heads, although some accounts claim it had many more, and one of these heads was immortal, making it an especially formidable opponent. Additionally, the Hydra's breath was poisonous, and its blood was lethal.

The Hydra resided in the swamps near the lake of Lerna, a desolate and eerie place shrouded in mist. The monster would emerge from its lair to ravage the countryside, killing livestock and poisoning the air and water with its toxic presence. To defeat this terrifying beast, Heracles set out with determination and a well-thought-out plan. He was accompanied by his nephew, Iolaus, who proved to be an invaluable ally in this endeavor.

Upon reaching the swampy region of Lerna, Heracles covered his mouth and nose to protect himself from the Hydra's poisonous fumes. He cautiously approached the creature's lair, a dark and foreboding cave partially submerged in the murky waters. Heracles knew that he had to draw the Hydra out of its hiding place to have any chance of defeating it. To accomplish this, he used flaming arrows to set the dense thicket around the cave on fire. The smoke and flames flushed the Hydra out, and the monstrous serpent emerged, hissing and snapping its many heads in fury.

The sight of the Hydra was terrifying. Its enormous, writhing body was covered in scales that glistened in the firelight, and its numerous heads moved with a menacing, serpentine grace. Heracles, armed with his trusty club and a sword, charged at the beast. He began by striking at the Hydra's heads, using his immense strength to sever them one by one. However, as soon as he cut off a head, two more would sprout from the stump, making the creature even more deadly. Heracles quickly realized that conventional methods would not suffice against this monstrous regenerative power.

In the midst of the battle, Heracles called upon Iolaus for assistance. Iolaus, understanding the gravity of the situation, retrieved a blazing torch. Together, they devised a new strategy to counter the Hydra's regenerative abilities. As Heracles severed each of the Hydra's heads, Iolaus immediately cauterized the stumps with the torch, preventing new heads from growing back. This coordinated effort required precision and speed, as the Hydra's heads moved rapidly and struck with deadly accuracy.

The battle raged on, with Heracles and Iolaus working in unison to overcome the monstrous foe. The Hydra's poisonous blood splattered the ground, and its hissing grew more frantic as it realized its regenerative power was being thwarted. Despite the creature's relentless attacks, Heracles's strength and Iolaus's quick thinking began to turn the tide of the battle.

Finally, Heracles faced the Hydra's central head, the one that was immortal. Knowing that this head could not be killed by conventional means, Heracles resorted to a different tactic. He seized the immortal head with his bare hands, using all his might to subdue it. He then grabbed a massive boulder and, with a tremendous effort, used it to pin the immortal head to the ground. To ensure that the head would never pose a threat again, Heracles buried it deep beneath the rock, trapping it for all eternity.

With the Hydra defeated, Heracles turned his attention to the creature's blood. Recognizing its deadly potency, he dipped his arrows into the Hydra's poisonous blood, imbuing them with lethal power. These arrows would later prove invaluable in Heracles's future labors and battles, giving him a fearsome advantage over his enemies.

Heracles and Iolaus then returned to Tiryns to present the proof of their victory to King Eurystheus. Upon seeing the severed heads of the Hydra and hearing the tale of how Heracles and Iolaus had overcome the beast, Eurystheus was both impressed and dismayed. He had hoped that the Hydra would be the end of Heracles, but the hero's resourcefulness and bravery had once again triumphed.

To discredit Heracles's accomplishment, Eurystheus, influenced by Hera, declared that the labor would not count because Heracles had received assistance from Iolaus. Despite this attempt to undermine his success, Heracles's reputation as an unstoppable hero only grew. His defeat of the Hydra was celebrated throughout Greece, further solidifying his legendary status.

The Third Labor: The Ceryneian Hind

For his third labor, Heracles was tasked with capturing the Ceryneian Hind, a sacred and elusive deer that belonged to the goddess Artemis. This particular labor was assigned by King Eurystheus under Hera's influence, designed to be a non-violent challenge that could still result in Heracles' failure. The hind was known for its remarkable speed and agility, making it nearly impossible to catch. Furthermore, the creature was protected by divine law, as it was sacred to Artemis, the goddess of the hunt and the wilderness. Any harm to the hind would incur the wrath of the goddess, adding another layer of difficulty to Heracles's task.

The Ceryneian Hind was a magnificent creature with golden antlers and hooves of bronze. It roamed freely through the hills and forests of Ceryneia in the northern Peloponnese, untouched by hunters and revered by the local population. The hind was said to be so swift that it could outrun an arrow in flight, making the prospect of capturing it daunting even for someone of Heracles's prowess.

Heracles set out on his quest, knowing that he needed to capture the hind without harming it, to avoid angering Artemis. His journey took him through dense forests, over rugged mountains, and across vast plains. He spent months tracking the hind, following its delicate hoofprints and learning its habits. During this time, Heracles honed his skills as a tracker, developing a deep understanding of the creature's movements and the terrain it favored.

For nearly a year, Heracles pursued the elusive hind, determined not to give up. He often caught glimpses of its golden antlers glinting in the sunlight or heard the soft rustle of leaves as it darted through the underbrush. Despite its elusiveness, Heracles remained patient, knowing that a hasty attempt could drive the creature deeper into the wilderness or provoke it into fleeing beyond his reach.

One early morning, as Heracles was navigating a particularly thick forest, he finally spotted the hind grazing by a clear stream. The creature's beauty was mesmerizing, and Heracles was careful not to startle it. He approached slowly, trying to close the distance without alarming the hind. When he was close enough, he drew an arrow and aimed for a spot that would immobilize the hind without causing serious harm. With great precision, Heracles released the arrow, which struck the hind between its forelegs, pinning it to the ground without drawing blood.

Heracles quickly approached the hind, speaking soothingly to calm the frightened animal. He gently bound its legs with rope, ensuring it would not injure itself in its attempts to escape. He then lifted the hind onto his shoulders, its golden antlers gleaming in the sunlight, and began the long journey back to Tiryns.

On his way back, Heracles encountered Artemis and her twin brother, Apollo. The goddess was furious at seeing her sacred hind in bonds, ready to unleash her wrath upon Heracles. However, Heracles, respectful and composed, explained the situation to Artemis. He recounted the command given by Eurystheus and emphasized his intention to return the hind unharmed as soon as he had shown it to the king.

Artemis, impressed by Heracles's honesty and reverence, agreed to let him proceed on the condition that the hind would indeed be returned safely. She allowed Heracles to continue, watching as he carried her sacred creature towards his destination. Heracles's respectful demeanor and clear explanation had defused a potentially dangerous situation, showcasing his ability to navigate not just physical challenges, but also the complex relationships between gods and mortals.

When Heracles finally arrived in Tiryns, Eurystheus was astonished to see the captured hind. The king had not expected Heracles to succeed, believing the task impossible. As per Artemis's condition, Heracles agreed to release the hind immediately after presenting it to Eurystheus. The moment Eurystheus had acknowledged the completion of the labor, Heracles unbound the hind and set it free. The creature bounded away with incredible speed, disappearing back into the wild, safe and unharmed.

This labor was significant not only for its physical demands but also for its requirement of tact and diplomacy. Heracles had managed to accomplish his task without causing harm, maintaining the delicate balance between honoring the commands of a mortal king and respecting the sanctity of the divine. The successful completion of this labor further solidified Heracles's reputation as a hero capable of overcoming not just brute challenges, but also those requiring patience, respect, and wisdom.

The Fourth Labor: The Erymanthian Boar

For his fourth labor, Heracles was tasked with capturing the Erymanthian Boar, a fearsome creature that roamed the slopes of Mount Erymanthos, wreaking havoc on the surrounding countryside. This monstrous boar was known for its enormous size, incredible strength, and vicious temperament. Its tusks were long and sharp, capable of goring both men and animals, and its presence instilled fear in the hearts of the local inhabitants. The task, as usual, was designed by King Eurystheus, with Hera's influence, to be perilous and difficult, hoping that this labor might finally lead to Heracles's demise.

Heracles set out for Mount Erymanthos, aware that capturing the boar alive would require both strength and strategy. The journey to the mountain was long and arduous, taking Heracles through dense forests and rugged terrain. Along the way, Heracles stopped to visit the centaur Pholus, an old friend who lived in a cave on the mountain. Pholus was known for his wisdom and hospitality, and Heracles hoped to gain some guidance and rest before confronting the boar.

Pholus welcomed Heracles warmly and offered him food and drink. As they shared a meal, Heracles noticed a large jar of wine in the cave. This wine, however, was not Pholus's to offer; it belonged to the community of centaurs and was meant to be shared only on special occasions. Heracles, unperturbed by this tradition, persuaded Pholus to open the jar and share the wine with him. As the rich aroma of the wine filled the cave, it attracted the attention of other centaurs living nearby.

The centaurs, smelling the wine, were enraged that it was being consumed without their consent. They stormed Pholus's cave, armed with rocks and tree branches, ready to reclaim their stolen treasure. A fierce battle ensued, with Heracles defending himself and Pholus against the enraged centaurs. Using his immense strength and skill, Heracles managed to drive them away, but not without causing significant chaos and injury.

During the skirmish, Heracles inadvertently killed several centaurs with his poisoned arrows, tipped with the deadly blood of the Lernaean Hydra. The remaining centaurs fled in fear, but one of the poisoned arrows struck Pholus, causing his death. Heracles was deeply saddened by the loss of his friend and gave him a proper burial before resuming his quest to capture the Erymanthian Boar.

With a heavy heart, Heracles continued his journey up the slopes of Mount Erymanthos, tracking the boar through the snow-covered terrain. The mountain was treacherous, with steep cliffs, dense forests, and deep snowdrifts making the hunt even more challenging. Heracles knew that the key to capturing the boar lay in exhausting it, as its strength and ferocity were unmatched.

For days, Heracles tracked the boar, studying its movements and patterns. He observed the creature from a distance, noting its favorite feeding grounds and resting places. Finally, Heracles devised a plan to drive the boar into a trap. He chose a narrow gorge as the ideal location for the ambush, where the steep cliffs would limit the boar's movements and provide an opportunity to capture it alive.

One cold morning, Heracles positioned himself near the gorge and let out a series of loud shouts and roars, mimicking the sounds of predators to drive the boar toward the trap. The startled boar, hearing the noise, charged through the forest in a frenzy, heading straight for the gorge. Heracles pursued the boar, carefully guiding it into the confined space.

As the boar entered the gorge, Heracles sprang into action. Using his immense strength, he wrestled the boar to the ground, avoiding its deadly tusks. The struggle was intense, with the boar thrashing and snarling, trying to break free.

Heracles held on, using his body weight and skill to subdue the beast. Finally, he managed to bind the boar's legs with sturdy ropes, securing it tightly.

With the Erymanthian Boar captured, Heracles prepared for the journey back to Tiryns. He hoisted the massive creature onto his shoulders, its weight a testament to his extraordinary strength. The return journey was long and challenging, but Heracles pressed on, determined to complete his task.

When Heracles arrived at Tiryns, King Eurystheus was once again filled with a mix of astonishment and fear. The sight of the captured boar, still alive and struggling, was both impressive and terrifying. In his usual display of cowardice, Eurystheus hid inside his large bronze jar, refusing to come out until Heracles had left the city.

The Fifth Labor: The Augean Stables

For his fifth labor, Heracles was assigned a task that seemed more suited for a menial worker than a heroic demigod: to clean the Augean Stables. King Eurystheus, under Hera's influence, designed this labor to be both humiliating and impossible. The Augean Stables belonged to King Augeas of Elis, and they housed a vast number of cattle. The stables had not been cleaned for over thirty years, and the accumulated filth presented a daunting challenge. Moreover, Augeas's cattle were said to be divinely healthy and exceptionally large, making the task even more formidable.

Heracles set out for Elis, determined to complete this labor as he had the previous ones, despite the degrading nature of the task. Upon arriving at Augeas's palace, he requested an audience with the king. Augeas, a wealthy and influential ruler, was initially skeptical of Heracles's intentions. Heracles proposed a wager to Augeas: if he could clean the stables in a single day, Augeas would reward him with a tenth of his cattle. Amused and confident that the task was impossible,

Augeas agreed, stipulating that Heracles could receive no assistance in his endeavor.

Heracles began by surveying the stables, which stretched as far as the eye could see. The sheer volume of manure and filth was overwhelming, and the stench was unbearable. Heracles knew that conventional methods of cleaning, such as shoveling, would be futile and would take months, if not years, to accomplish. He needed to devise a plan that would allow him to complete the task within the allotted time.

Drawing on his ingenuity and understanding of the natural world, Heracles conceived a bold plan to use the power of the nearby rivers. The Alpheus and Peneus rivers flowed through the region, and Heracles realized that if he could divert their courses, he could harness their currents to wash away the accumulated filth in the stables. This method would not only clean the stables swiftly but also demonstrate his intelligence and resourcefulness.

Heracles began by constructing a series of trenches and channels to redirect the flow of the rivers. Using his immense strength, he moved large boulders and earth to create a path that would lead the waters directly through the stables. This required precise calculations and an understanding of hydraulics, as the rivers needed to be diverted without causing flooding or damaging the surrounding areas.

As Heracles worked, the inhabitants of Elis watched in awe and curiosity. Many doubted that his plan would succeed, but Heracles remained focused and determined. By midday, the trenches were complete, and Heracles stood ready to execute his plan. With a final, mighty effort, he breached the riverbanks, allowing the waters of the Alpheus and Peneus to surge through the channels he had created.

The rushing waters cascaded through the Augean Stables, carrying away years of accumulated filth and manure. The force of the currents scoured the floors and walls, leaving the stables remarkably clean in a matter of hours. Heracles supervised the process, ensuring that the flow remained controlled and that no further damage was done to the structures.

By the end of the day, the Augean Stables were not only clean but gleaming. Heracles had accomplished what seemed impossible, using his intellect and brawn to achieve his goal. He approached King Augeas to claim his reward, confident in the success of his labor.

However, Augeas, realizing the magnitude of Heracles's achievement and fearing the loss of his valuable cattle, reneged on their agreement. He argued that Heracles had only succeeded by using the rivers and had not actually cleaned the stables by hand, as implied by the challenge. Augeas further claimed that Heracles had acted under orders from Eurystheus and therefore was not entitled to any reward.

Outraged by this deceit, Heracles demanded justice. He took his case to a tribunal, composed of Augeas's son Phyleus and other local nobles. Phyleus, who admired Heracles and was appalled by his father's dishonesty, testified in Heracles's favor. The tribunal ruled that Augeas must honor his agreement and pay Heracles the promised reward. Enraged by the verdict, Augeas banished both Heracles and Phyleus from Elis, refusing to comply with the ruling.

Heracles, though denied his rightful reward, had successfully completed the labor set by Eurystheus. He returned to Tiryns, where Eurystheus, ever resentful and influenced by Hera, refused to count the labor, claiming that Heracles had been compensated for his work. Despite this setback, Heracles's reputation continued to grow. His clever solution to the Augean Stables problem showcased not only his physical prowess but also his strategic mind.

The Sixth Labor: The Stymphalian Birds

For his sixth labor, Heracles was tasked with driving away the Stymphalian Birds, a flock of deadly creatures that had taken up residence in the marshes near Lake Stymphalia in Arcadia. These birds were no ordinary avians; they were said to have been bred by Ares, the god of war, and possessed metallic feathers that they could launch like arrows. Their beaks were sharp as swords, and their talons were capable of rending flesh and armor alike. The Stymphalian Birds terrorized the local population, destroying crops, killing livestock, and attacking anyone who ventured too close to their lair.

King Eurystheus, influenced by Hera, assigned this labor to Heracles in the hope that the hero would be overwhelmed by the sheer number of these vicious birds. The task required not only physical prowess but also ingenuity, as Heracles had to find a way to deal with a vast number of fast-moving, airborne adversaries.

Heracles traveled to Arcadia, where he began his search for the marshes of Lake Stymphalia. The journey through the dense forests and rugged terrain was arduous, but Heracles was determined to complete his task. Upon reaching the marshes, he quickly realized the difficulty of the labor. The area was a vast, waterlogged expanse, with thick reeds and dense undergrowth providing perfect cover for the birds.

The Stymphalian Birds were elusive, and Heracles knew that confronting them directly in their marshy habitat would be futile. As he pondered his approach, Athena, the goddess of wisdom and warfare, appeared to him. Recognizing the challenge Heracles faced, she provided him with a pair of bronze castanets, also known as krotala, crafted by Hephaestus, the god of blacksmiths and fire. These noisemakers, when clashed together, would create a cacophony loud enough to frighten the birds into flight, forcing them out of their hiding places.

Armed with this divine gift, Heracles approached the marshes at dawn, when the birds were typically less active. He positioned himself at the edge of the water, where he could easily spot the birds as they took to the air. With a deep breath, he clashed the bronze castanets together, producing a sound that echoed across the marshes like thunder.

The noise startled the Stymphalian Birds, and they erupted from the reeds in a chaotic flurry of metallic wings and sharp cries. The sky darkened as the birds took flight, their numbers so vast that they blotted out the sun. Heracles, prepared for this moment, seized his bow and a quiver of arrows dipped in the poisonous blood of the Lernaean Hydra, which he had obtained during his second labor.

With precise aim and unerring skill, Heracles began to shoot the birds out of the sky. His poisoned arrows struck true, and each bird that was hit fell dead into the marshes below. Despite the birds' speed and the danger of their razor-sharp feathers, Heracles remained calm and focused, systematically thinning their numbers. The birds, panicked by the noise and the relentless assault, began to scatter in all directions.

As the battle continued, the flock of Stymphalian Birds grew smaller and smaller. Some birds, recognizing the futility of fighting the hero, fled the area entirely, seeking refuge in distant lands. Heracles pursued the remaining birds, ensuring that none would return to terrorize the region. By the end of the day, the marshes of Lake Stymphalia were littered with the bodies of the fallen birds, and the sky was clear.

Heracles, having successfully driven away or killed the Stymphalian Birds, took a moment to rest and reflect on his victory. The labor had tested not only his martial skills but also his ability to adapt to new challenges and use the tools provided by the gods. The people of Arcadia, grateful for their deliverance, hailed Heracles as a hero and celebrated his triumph.

Returning to Tiryns, Heracles presented the proof of his success to King Eurystheus. The king, ever fearful of the hero's growing legend, reluctantly acknowledged the completion of the labor. Once again, Eurystheus was forced to concede that Heracles had overcome an insurmountable challenge, further solidifying the hero's reputation.

The Seventh Labor: The Cretan Bull

For his seventh labor, Heracles was tasked with capturing the Cretan Bull, a magnificent and formidable creature that had been wreaking havoc on the island of Crete. This labor, like the others, was assigned by King Eurystheus under the influence of Hera, who hoped that the monstrous bull would prove too much for Heracles to handle. The bull was known for its immense strength and ferocity, and its capture would require not only Heracles's physical prowess but also his strategic thinking and determination.

The Cretan Bull had a storied history. It was originally sent by Poseidon, the god of the sea, as a gift to King Minos of Crete, who was supposed to sacrifice the bull to honor the god. However, Minos, captivated by the bull's beauty and majesty, decided to keep it for himself and sacrificed a lesser bull instead. Angered by this deceit, Poseidon cursed the bull, causing it to become wild and uncontrollable. The bull rampaged across Crete, destroying crops, flattening homes, and terrorizing the people. It was also infamous for fathering the Minotaur, a monstrous creature with the body of a man and the head of a bull, born from Minos's queen, Pasiphae.

Heracles set sail for Crete, determined to capture the bull alive and bring it back to Tiryns. Upon arriving on the island, he sought an audience with King Minos to inform him of his mission. King Minos, who was eager to rid his land of the destructive creature, welcomed Heracles and offered any assistance he might need. Heracles, however, preferred to face the challenge alone, relying on his own strength and skill.

Heracles began his search for the Cretan Bull, traveling across the island and speaking with the local inhabitants who had witnessed the bull's rampages. He gathered information about the bull's last known whereabouts and its behavior, learning that it frequented the open fields and pastures near the northern coast of Crete. Heracles spent several days tracking the bull, following the trail of destruction it left in its wake.

One morning, as Heracles was scouting a particularly devastated area, he spotted the Cretan Bull grazing in a distant meadow. The bull was indeed a magnificent sight, with a muscular build, a shining white coat, and horns that glinted in the sunlight. Heracles approached cautiously, knowing that any sudden movements could provoke the bull into a deadly charge.

When he was close enough, Heracles called out to the bull, drawing its attention. The bull, sensing a challenge, snorted and pawed the ground, preparing to charge. Heracles stood his ground, waiting for the right moment. As the bull charged toward him, Heracles sidestepped with incredible agility and leaped onto its back. The bull bucked and thrashed, trying to throw Heracles off, but the hero held on tightly, using his immense strength to stay mounted.

A fierce struggle ensued as Heracles wrestled with the powerful creature. He wrapped his arms around the bull's neck, using his weight to slow it down and tire it out. The bull continued to fight, but Heracles's grip was unrelenting. Gradually, the bull's movements grew weaker as it exhausted itself, and Heracles was able to bring it under control.

With the bull subdued, Heracles bound its legs with rope, ensuring it could not escape. He then led the bull back to the palace of King Minos, where the people of Crete gathered to witness the incredible sight. The islanders cheered and celebrated Heracles's success, grateful that the terror of the Cretan Bull was finally over.

King Minos, impressed by Heracles's feat, offered him hospitality and thanked him for ridding Crete of the destructive creature. Heracles, however, had no time to rest, as he needed to deliver the bull to King Eurystheus in Tiryns. He arranged for a ship to transport the bull across the sea, ensuring that the creature was securely bound for the journey.

The voyage back to Tiryns was uneventful, and Heracles arrived safely with the captured bull. When he presented the Cretan Bull to Eurystheus, the king was once again filled with a mix of astonishment and dread. The sight of the powerful beast, subdued and under Heracles's control, was both impressive and intimidating. As usual, Eurystheus tried to distance himself from the dangerous creature, ordering Heracles to release the bull outside the city.

Heracles complied, setting the bull free. The Cretan Bull wandered north, eventually crossing the Isthmus of Corinth and causing havoc in the region of Marathon. There, it became known as the Marathonian Bull, continuing its legacy of destruction until it was ultimately killed by the hero Theseus.

The Eighth Labor: The Mares of Diomedes

For his eighth labor, Heracles was tasked with capturing the Mares of Diomedes, a quartet of man-eating horses owned by the Thracian king Diomedes. These mares, known for their ferocity and insatiable appetite for human flesh, were a symbol of Diomedes's cruelty and power. Eurystheus, under Hera's influence, believed that this labor would surely bring about Heracles's downfall, given the deadly nature of the beasts.

Diomedes, a son of Ares, the god of war, was a brutal and tyrannical ruler. His mares were kept tethered to a bronze manger in a stable fortified by iron bars. The stables were located on the coast of the Black Sea, in a region known as Thrace.

These horses were fed on the flesh of Diomedes's enemies and anyone who dared to defy him, making them wild and uncontrollable.

Heracles set out for Thrace, accompanied by a small band of loyal companions, including his close friend Abderus. Upon reaching the kingdom of Diomedes, Heracles devised a plan to capture the mares. He decided to approach the task under the cover of night, hoping to take the horses by surprise and avoid a direct confrontation with Diomedes and his men.

As night fell, Heracles and his companions approached the stables. The air was thick with tension, and the smell of blood and death emanated from the area. Heracles instructed his companions to stand guard while he entered the stables. Using his immense strength, he pried open the iron bars and untethered the mares. The horses, sensing freedom, reared and kicked, but Heracles managed to calm them with his commanding presence.

Just as Heracles was about to lead the mares out of the stables, a commotion arose. Diomedes and his soldiers, alerted to the intrusion, surrounded the stables. A fierce battle ensued, with Heracles and his companions fighting bravely against the Thracians. Heracles, wielding his club and displaying unparalleled strength and skill, fought his way through the enemy ranks.

During the battle, Heracles entrusted the mares to Abderus, instructing him to hold them while he dealt with Diomedes. Abderus, though brave, was no match for the wild and powerful mares. The horses, driven by their insatiable hunger, turned on Abderus and devoured him. Heracles, upon realizing what had happened, was filled with rage and sorrow.

Determined to avenge his friend, Heracles fought with renewed fury. He confronted Diomedes and overpowered him, dragging the tyrant to the stables. In a fitting act of poetic justice, Heracles fed Diomedes to his own man-eating horses, sating their hunger and calming their savage nature. With Diomedes dead, the remaining Thracian soldiers fled in fear, leaving Heracles and his companions victorious.

Heracles, though saddened by the loss of Abderus, knew he had to complete his labor. He took control of the now-docile mares and led them away from the stables. In honor of his fallen friend, Heracles founded the city of Abdera near the site of the stables, ensuring that Abderus's bravery would not be forgotten.

The journey back to Tiryns was arduous, as the mares, though calmed, were still powerful and difficult to manage. Heracles and his companions took turns keeping watch over the horses, ensuring they remained under control. Along the way, they encountered various challenges, including harsh weather and treacherous terrain, but Heracles's determination and leadership saw them through.

Upon reaching Tiryns, Heracles presented the Mares of Diomedes to King Eurystheus. The king, as always, was filled with a mixture of awe and fear at Heracles's success. Eurystheus had the mares dedicated to Hera, hoping to placate the goddess and keep the dangerous creatures away from himself. The mares were eventually set free and roamed the plains of Argos, where they were said to have met their end at the hands of wild beasts.

The Ninth Labor: The Belt of Hippolyta

For his ninth labor, Heracles was tasked with obtaining the belt of Hippolyta, the queen of the Amazons. The belt, also known as the Girdle of Hippolyta, was a symbol of her authority and had been given to her by Ares, the god of war. King Eurystheus, under Hera's influence, assigned this labor with the hope that Heracles would face insurmountable challenges among the fierce warrior women. Eurystheus desired the belt as a gift for his daughter, Admete, and saw this labor as an opportunity to rid himself of Heracles once and for all.

The Amazons were a formidable tribe of warrior women known for their exceptional combat skills and matriarchal society. They lived in the region near the Black Sea, in a land called Themiscyra. The Amazons were feared and respected throughout the ancient world for their martial prowess and their ability to defend their territory against any invaders.

Heracles assembled a team of trusted companions, including the hero Theseus, to aid him on this challenging mission. Together, they set sail for Themiscyra, navigating treacherous waters and encountering various perils along the way. The journey was long and arduous, but Heracles and his companions remained steadfast in their determination to complete the labor.

Upon reaching the land of the Amazons, Heracles sent a messenger to request an audience with Queen Hippolyta. To his surprise, Hippolyta welcomed him and his companions warmly. She had heard of Heracles's legendary exploits and admired his strength and courage. When Heracles explained his mission and requested the belt, Hippolyta, impressed by his honesty and valor, agreed to give it to him willingly.

However, Hera, ever determined to thwart Heracles, disguised herself as one of the Amazons and spread rumors among the tribe that Heracles and his men were there to abduct their queen. The Amazons, stirred into a frenzy by Hera's deceit, armed themselves and prepared for battle, believing that they needed to defend their queen and their honor.

As Heracles and Hippolyta were negotiating the terms of the belt's exchange, the Amazons, led by Penthesilea, charged towards the camp, weapons drawn and ready for combat. Heracles, seeing the approaching warriors and realizing the misunderstanding, tried to reason with them, but the situation quickly escalated into a fierce battle.

Heracles and his companions fought bravely against the Amazons, displaying their martial skills and strength. Heracles, wielding his mighty club and wearing the lion's pelt from his first labor, was a formidable sight on the battlefield. Despite the chaos, he continued to seek out Hippolyta, hoping to resolve the conflict without further bloodshed.

In the midst of the battle, Heracles confronted Hippolyta, who was torn between her loyalty to her tribe and her admiration for the hero. Realizing that Hera's treachery had caused the conflict, Hippolyta called for a ceasefire and addressed her warriors. She explained that Heracles's intentions were honorable and that she had agreed to give him the belt willingly.

The Amazons, though still wary, respected their queen's decision and lowered their weapons. Hippolyta, true to her word, presented the belt to Heracles as a token of peace and respect. The tension on the battlefield eased as both sides recognized the mutual respect and honor in their actions.

With the belt in his possession, Heracles thanked Hippolyta for her understanding and cooperation. He and his companions prepared to leave Themiscyra, grateful for the peaceful resolution of what could have been a disastrous conflict. The journey back to Tiryns was filled with relief and satisfaction, as Heracles knew he had completed another challenging labor through a combination of strength, diplomacy, and perseverance.

Upon returning to Tiryns, Heracles presented the belt to King Eurystheus, who, despite his jealousy and resentment, had to acknowledge Heracles's success. Eurystheus handed the belt to his daughter, Admete, fulfilling his promise and further cementing Heracles's reputation as a hero capable of overcoming even the most formidable challenges.

The Tenth Labor: The Cattle of Geryon

For his tenth labor, Heracles was tasked with a perilous journey to the distant land of Erytheia to capture the cattle of Geryon, a fearsome giant with three bodies and a single pair of legs. Each of Geryon's three bodies had its own set of arms and heads, making him a formidable adversary. The cattle, known for their striking red color, were guarded not only by Geryon but also by his two-headed dog, Orthrus, and the herdsman Eurytion. This labor, assigned by King Eurystheus under Hera's influence, was designed to test Heracles's endurance, strength, and strategic prowess.

The journey to Erytheia was long and fraught with danger. Heracles set out from Tiryns, traveling through the Mediterranean and across various lands, encountering numerous challenges along the way. One of the most significant obstacles he faced was crossing the vast Libyan desert. The scorching heat and relentless sun made the journey nearly unbearable, but Heracles, drawing on his immense strength and determination, pressed on.

As he crossed the desert, Heracles encountered a giant named Antaeus, the son of Gaia (the Earth) and Poseidon. Antaeus was known for his invincibility, as he derived his strength from his mother, the Earth. Each time he touched the ground, his power was renewed. Antaeus challenged Heracles to a wrestling match, confident in his ability to defeat the hero. Heracles, aware of Antaeus's secret, lifted the giant off the ground, breaking his connection to the Earth, and crushed him in a powerful embrace. With Antaeus defeated, Heracles continued his journey.

As Heracles neared the straits that would later be known as the Pillars of Heracles (modern-day Strait of Gibraltar), he encountered another challenge: the vast expanse of the ocean. Determined to reach Erytheia, Heracles constructed two massive pillars to mark the edge of the known world, symbolizing his strength and perseverance. He then borrowed the golden cup of Helios, the sun god, which Helios used to sail across the sky each day. Heracles used the cup to traverse the sea, finally reaching the island of Erytheia.

Upon arriving in Erytheia, Heracles immediately set out to locate the cattle of Geryon. He first encountered Orthrus, the two-headed dog, who fiercely guarded the herd. With a swift and powerful strike, Heracles dispatched the beast. Next, he faced Eurytion, the herdsman, who attempted to protect the cattle from the intruding hero. Heracles defeated Eurytion with ease, leaving the path clear to the cattle.

However, the commotion attracted the attention of Geryon, who quickly armed himself and confronted Heracles. The sight of the three-bodied giant, each wielding weapons and armor, was daunting, but Heracles remained undeterred. A fierce battle ensued, with Heracles using his immense strength and agility to evade Geryon's attacks. As the fight continued, Heracles seized an opportunity and drew his bow, firing a single, deadly arrow tipped with the poisonous blood of the Lernaean Hydra. The arrow struck Geryon in one of his three hearts, killing him instantly.

With Geryon defeated, Heracles gathered the cattle and began the long journey back to Tiryns. Herding the cattle across such vast distances presented its own set of challenges. Along the way, he encountered various obstacles and enemies, including hostile tribes and natural barriers. One notable challenge occurred when the god Poseidon, seeking to avenge the death of his son Antaeus, sent a swarm of gadflies to torment the cattle. The flies caused the herd to scatter, but Heracles, with great effort, managed to round them up and continue his journey.

Heracles also encountered the thief Cacus in Italy, who attempted to steal some of the cattle. Cacus, a fire-breathing giant, hid the stolen cattle in his cave. Heracles tracked the thief down and engaged him in a fierce battle. Using his incredible strength, Heracles overpowered Cacus and retrieved the stolen cattle, ensuring the herd remained intact.

Finally, after many months of arduous travel and countless trials, Heracles arrived in Tiryns with the cattle of Geryon. King Eurystheus, as always, was both impressed and fearful of Heracles's achievements. To demonstrate his success,

Heracles presented the red cattle to Eurystheus, fulfilling the terms of the labor. Eurystheus, reluctant to keep the cattle due to their divine and fearsome origins, sacrificed them to Hera, hoping to appease the goddess and mitigate any further divine wrath.

The Eleventh Labor: The Apples of the Hesperides

For his eleventh labor, Heracles was tasked with obtaining the golden apples of the Hesperides, which were sacred to Hera. These apples grew in a garden at the western edge of the world, tended by the Hesperides, the nymph daughters of Atlas, and guarded by the fearsome dragon Ladon, a serpent-like creature with a hundred heads. The apples were a wedding gift from Gaia to Hera and Zeus, symbolizing eternal youth and immortality. This labor, assigned by King Eurystheus, was intended to be nearly impossible, requiring Heracles to overcome both physical and intellectual challenges.

Heracles set out on his journey, knowing that the location of the garden was shrouded in mystery. His quest began with seeking information from those who might know the way. He traveled through various lands, consulting oracles and wise men, but their answers were often cryptic and unhelpful. Determined, Heracles decided to seek out the shape-shifting sea god, Proteus, who was known for his vast knowledge and ability to see the future.

Finding Proteus was no easy task, as the god was elusive and often changed his form to avoid capture. Heracles waited by the shore, disguising himself and ambushing Proteus when he emerged from the sea. Heracles grappled with Proteus, holding him tightly as the god shifted into various forms, including a lion, a serpent, and a torrent of water. Finally, Proteus, unable to escape Heracles's grasp, agreed to answer his questions. He revealed that the garden of the Hesperides was located beyond the land of the Hyperboreans, at the edge of the world, and that only the Titan Atlas could help him retrieve the apples.

Armed with this knowledge, Heracles resumed his journey, traveling through the northern regions and enduring harsh climates and difficult terrain. Along the way, he encountered numerous challenges, including hostile tribes and wild beasts. Each obstacle tested Heracles's strength and resilience, but he pressed on, driven by his determination to complete his labor.

As he approached the western edge of the world, Heracles encountered Prometheus, the Titan who had been bound to a rock by Zeus as punishment for giving fire to humanity. Each day, an eagle would come to devour Prometheus's liver, only for it to regenerate overnight, subjecting him to eternal torment. Heracles, moved by the Titan's suffering, decided to free Prometheus. Using his strength, he shattered the chains that bound Prometheus and killed the eagle with a single arrow. In gratitude, Prometheus advised Heracles on how to obtain the golden apples, suggesting that he seek the assistance of Atlas, who held up the sky nearby.

Heracles found Atlas, the Titan condemned to bear the weight of the heavens on his shoulders. Explaining his mission, Heracles offered to temporarily take Atlas's burden if the Titan would retrieve the apples from his daughters' garden. Relieved at the prospect of a temporary reprieve, Atlas agreed and instructed Heracles on how to support the sky. Heracles positioned himself under the celestial weight, allowing Atlas to set off for the garden.

Atlas approached the garden of the Hesperides, where his daughters, the nymphs, welcomed him. Using his knowledge of the garden and his familiarity with Ladon, Atlas managed to lull the dragon to sleep and plucked the golden apples from the tree. Upon his return, Atlas, feeling the freedom from his eternal burden, was reluctant to resume his position. He suggested that he deliver the apples to Eurystheus himself, intending to leave Heracles with the weight of the heavens forever.

Heracles, realizing Atlas's intention, cleverly agreed but asked Atlas to hold the sky for a moment while he adjusted his cloak to make the weight more comfortable. Atlas, not suspecting any trickery, took back the heavens. With Atlas once again bearing the celestial burden, Heracles swiftly gathered the golden apples and made his way back to Greece.

The journey back was no less arduous, but Heracles's resolve was unshakable. He navigated treacherous landscapes and faced numerous dangers, always keeping his goal in sight. Upon his return to Tiryns, Heracles presented the golden apples to King Eurystheus. The king, as always, was both impressed and unnerved by Heracles's success. Knowing the apples belonged to the gods, Eurystheus decided to return them to Athena, who subsequently brought them back to the garden of the Hesperides.

The Twelfth Labor: Cerberus

The twelfth and final labor assigned to Heracles was perhaps the most daunting of all: to capture Cerberus, the ferocious three-headed guard dog of the Underworld. Cerberus, a monstrous offspring of the primordial creatures Typhon and Echidna, was tasked with preventing the dead from leaving and the living from entering Hades. This labor was designed by King Eurystheus and Hera to be an insurmountable challenge, one that would test Heracles's courage, strength, and resilience to their limits.

To begin this perilous journey, Heracles first needed to prepare himself for the descent into the Underworld, a realm where mortals were not meant to tread. He traveled to Eleusis, where he sought initiation into the Eleusinian Mysteries, the secret religious rites dedicated to Demeter and Persephone. These rites were believed to offer protection and favor from the gods of the Underworld, as well as a promise of a blessed afterlife. Heracles's initiation into these mysteries would ensure he had the spiritual fortitude to face the dangers that lay ahead.

With the blessings of the Eleusinian Mysteries, Heracles made his way to the entrance of the Underworld, located at Taenarum, a cave at the southern tip of the Peloponnese. As he descended into the dark, foreboding depths, Heracles encountered a series of spectral figures and tormented souls. The eerie silence and oppressive atmosphere tested his resolve, but Heracles pressed on, his mind focused on the task at hand.

Upon reaching the river Styx, the boundary between the world of the living and the dead, Heracles was met by Charon, the grim ferryman who transported souls across the river. Charon, recognizing Heracles as a living being, was initially reluctant to ferry him across. However, Heracles's divine heritage and his initiation into the Eleusinian Mysteries persuaded Charon to grant him passage. The ferryman rowed Heracles across the dark, swirling waters of the Styx, bringing him closer to his goal.

As he journeyed deeper into the Underworld, Heracles encountered the shades of various heroes and mortals. Among them was the spirit of Meleager, a renowned hero who had died prematurely. Meleager, moved by Heracles's presence, revealed that his sister Deianira was of marriageable age and would make a suitable bride for the hero. Heracles, touched by Meleager's story, promised to seek out Deianira upon his return to the living world.

Heracles then approached the palace of Hades and Persephone, the rulers of the Underworld. He sought an audience with them to request permission to take Cerberus to the surface. Hades, impressed by Heracles's bravery and respectful demeanor, agreed to his request, but on one condition: Heracles must capture Cerberus without using any weapons, relying solely on his strength and courage. Heracles accepted the challenge, aware that this final labor would require every ounce of his power and determination.

Hades led Heracles to the gates of Tartarus, the deepest part of the Underworld, where Cerberus stood guard. The monstrous dog, with its three snarling heads, a serpent for a tail, and venomous snakes protruding from its back, was a fearsome sight. Each of Cerberus's heads snapped and growled, its eyes glowing with a menacing fire. Heracles steeled himself for the confrontation, knowing that failure was not an option.

With great caution, Heracles approached Cerberus, his every movement calculated to avoid provoking the beast prematurely. The air was thick with tension as Cerberus fixed its three pairs of eyes on the hero. Then, with a burst of speed and agility, Heracles lunged at the monstrous dog, wrapping his powerful arms around the central head and neck. Cerberus thrashed and roared, its other heads snapping at Heracles in a frenzy, but the hero held firm.

Using his immense strength, Heracles tightened his grip, wrestling Cerberus to the ground. The struggle was intense, with Heracles enduring bites and strikes from the serpent tail and the snapping jaws of the other heads. Blood and sweat mingled as Heracles fought to subdue the beast, his muscles straining with the effort. Gradually, through sheer force of will and power, he managed to overpower Cerberus, binding the creature with chains forged from the shadows of the Underworld.

With Cerberus subdued, Heracles began the arduous journey back to the surface, dragging the massive beast through the dark passages and across the Styx. Charon, once again persuaded by Heracles's determination and divine favor, ferried him back across the river. As Heracles emerged from the depths of the Underworld, the light of the living world was blinding, and the weight of his final labor settled upon him.

Heracles led Cerberus to Tiryns, where King Eurystheus awaited the outcome of the labor with a mixture of dread and disbelief. The sight of Heracles, victorious and accompanied by the monstrous guard dog of the Underworld, struck fear into Eurystheus's heart. The cowardly king once again sought refuge in his bronze jar, unwilling to face the hero directly.

Having completed the twelfth labor, Heracles honored his agreement with Hades and returned Cerberus to the Underworld, ensuring that the balance between the realms of the living and the dead remained undisturbed. This final labor, more than any other, demonstrated Heracles's unparalleled strength, courage, and resilience. He had ventured into the realm of the dead, faced its guardian, and emerged triumphant, solidifying his place as one of the greatest heroes in Greek mythology.

The successful completion of the twelfth labor marked the end of Heracles's servitude to Eurystheus and fulfilled the terms of his penance. Each labor had tested different aspects of his character, from physical strength to strategic thinking and compassion. Through these trials, Heracles had proven himself time and again, earning the admiration and respect of gods and mortals alike.

CHAPTER 9: THE TROJAN WAR

The seeds of the Trojan War were sown long before the first spear was thrown or the first ship set sail. The origins of this epic conflict can be traced back to the wedding of Peleus, a mortal king, and Thetis, a sea nymph. All the gods and goddesses were invited to this grand celebration, save for Eris, the goddess of discord. Angered by her exclusion, Eris decided to wreak havoc on the festivities by tossing a golden apple into the crowd, inscribed with the words "To the fairest."

Three powerful goddesses—Hera, Athena, and Aphrodite—each claimed the apple for themselves, leading to a fierce argument. Unable to resolve the dispute, they turned to Zeus, the king of the gods, for judgment. Zeus, not wanting to incur the wrath of any of the goddesses, delegated the task to Paris, a prince of Troy known for his fairness and beauty.

Paris was promised rewards by each goddess in exchange for choosing her as the fairest. Hera offered him power and kingship over all of Asia, Athena promised wisdom and skill in battle, and Aphrodite tempted him with the most beautiful woman in the world as his wife. Swayed by the promise of love, Paris awarded the golden apple to Aphrodite.

The most beautiful woman in the world was Helen, the wife of Menelaus, the king of Sparta. With Aphrodite's help, Paris traveled to Sparta, where he was welcomed as a guest. However, Paris betrayed Menelaus's hospitality by abducting

Helen and taking her back to Troy. This act of treachery would spark a conflict that would engulf both Greece and Troy in a devastating war.

When Menelaus discovered that his wife had been taken by Paris, he was furious and sought the aid of his brother, Agamemnon, the powerful king of Mycenae. Agamemnon, eager to assert his dominance and avenge the insult to his family, called upon all the Greek kings and heroes to honor their oaths, sworn years earlier, to defend the marriage of Helen and Menelaus. These oaths had been taken when Helen's hand was contested by many suitors, and they now bound the Greek leaders to take up arms against Troy.

Among the greatest of these leaders were:

Achilles, the mightiest of the Greek warriors, the son of Peleus and Thetis, who was invulnerable except for his heel.

Odysseus, the cunning and resourceful king of Ithaca, known for his intelligence and wit.

Ajax the Great, a towering warrior known for his strength and courage.

Diomedes, a formidable fighter who would prove his valor on the battlefield.

Nestor, the wise and aged king of Pylos, who served as a counselor to the younger warriors.

Agamemnon assembled a vast fleet of more than a thousand ships, and the Greek army, known as the Achaeans, set sail for Troy. However, before they could depart, Agamemnon offended the goddess Artemis by killing a sacred deer. In her anger, Artemis caused the winds to cease, trapping the Greek fleet at Aulis. To appease the goddess, Agamemnon was forced to make a terrible sacrifice: his own daughter, Iphigenia. With a heavy heart, Agamemnon consented, and once the sacrifice was made, the winds returned, allowing the fleet to continue its journey to Troy.

The Greek forces arrived at the shores of Troy and laid siege to the city, marking the beginning of a ten-year conflict. The city of Troy, ruled by King Priam, was a formidable fortress, well-defended by its high walls and valiant warriors. Among the Trojan defenders were Hector, Priam's eldest son and the greatest of the Trojan heroes, and Aeneas, a noble warrior who would later become the founder of Rome.

The war raged on, with neither side able to gain a decisive advantage. The gods themselves took sides in the conflict, with Hera, Athena, and Poseidon supporting the Greeks, while Aphrodite, Apollo, and Ares favored the Trojans. Zeus, attempting to maintain a balance, often intervened to prevent either side from achieving complete victory.

Throughout the war, many battles were fought, and many heroes distinguished themselves. Achilles, in particular, became a legend on the battlefield, cutting down countless Trojan warriors. However, a quarrel between Achilles and Agamemnon nearly led to disaster for the Greeks. Agamemnon, in a show of arrogance, took Briseis, a captive woman and Achilles's prize of war, from him. Enraged by this insult, Achilles withdrew from the fighting, refusing to aid the Greeks further.

Without Achilles, the tide of the war turned in favor of the Trojans. Hector led a fierce assault on the Greek camp, even setting fire to some of their ships. The Greeks were on the brink of defeat, and it seemed that Troy might emerge victorious.

Desperate to save the Greek forces, Patroclus, Achilles's closest companion and dear friend, donned Achilles's armor and led the Myrmidons into battle. Believing that Achilles had returned to the fight, the Trojans were initially driven back. However, Patroclus's ruse was soon discovered, and Hector, the greatest of the Trojan warriors, confronted him in battle. The two fought fiercely, but Hector ultimately slew Patroclus, believing he had killed Achilles himself.

When the news of Patroclus's death reached Achilles, he was overcome with grief and rage. His sorrow was so deep that he swore to avenge Patroclus, even if it meant his own death. Achilles reconciled with Agamemnon and returned to the battlefield, determined to confront Hector and bring about his downfall.

Clad in new armor forged by the god Hephaestus, Achilles entered the fray with a fury unmatched by any other warrior. He slaughtered countless Trojans in his pursuit of Hector, driving the Trojan forces back within the walls of their city. Finally, Achilles confronted Hector outside the gates of Troy.

The duel between Achilles and Hector was one of the most fateful moments of the war. Hector, knowing his fate was sealed, faced Achilles with courage and honor. The two fought a fierce battle, but Achilles's strength and skill were too much for Hector. With a final, devastating blow, Achilles struck down Hector, and in his rage, he desecrated Hector's body by dragging it behind his chariot around the walls of Troy.

Achilles's wrath was so great that he refused to return Hector's body to the Trojans for burial, a decision that deeply grieved King Priam. Moved by the gods, Priam ventured into the Greek camp to plead with Achilles for the return of his son's body. Touched by Priam's courage and sorrow, Achilles finally relented and returned Hector's body to the Trojans, allowing them to perform the proper funeral rites.

The death of Hector marked a turning point in the war. Although the Trojans continued to resist, they knew that without Hector, their greatest defender, the end was near. The Greeks, however, struggled to breach the walls of Troy, and it seemed that the war might drag on indefinitely.

It was at this critical moment that Odysseus devised a cunning plan that would lead to the downfall of Troy. He proposed building a large wooden horse, hollowed out to conceal a group of Greek warriors inside. The Greeks would then pretend to abandon the siege, leaving the horse as a supposed offering to the gods for a safe journey home.

The plan was put into action, and the Greeks built the enormous horse, which became known as the Trojan Horse. The bravest and most skilled Greek warriors, including Odysseus, Menelaus, and others, hid inside the hollow structure, while the rest of the Greek forces burned their camp and sailed away to a nearby island, out of sight of Troy.

When the Trojans discovered the deserted Greek camp and the massive wooden horse, they were perplexed. Some, like the priest Laocoön, warned that the horse was a trick, and urged the Trojans to destroy it. However, the Trojans were divided in their opinions, and ultimately, they decided to bring the horse into the city as a trophy and a symbol of their victory.

That night, as the Trojans celebrated their apparent triumph, the Greek warriors inside the horse emerged and opened the gates of Troy. The Greek army, which had sailed back under cover of darkness, stormed the city. The Trojans, caught off guard and unprepared for battle, were slaughtered. Troy was sacked and burned, its people either killed or taken as slaves. King Priam was slain, and the city that had stood strong for ten years of war was reduced to ruins.

The fall of Troy marked the end of the war, but the aftermath of the conflict brought further tragedy and suffering to both the Greeks and the Trojans. Helen, whose abduction had sparked the war, was taken back to Sparta by Menelaus. Despite the years of conflict, she was forgiven by her husband and returned to her former life as queen.

The Greek heroes who had survived the war faced their own challenges as they attempted to return home. Many of them were cursed by the gods for their actions during the war, leading to long and perilous journeys. Odysseus, in particular, would face a ten-year odyssey filled with trials and tribulations before he could finally return to Ithaca.

Achilles, the greatest of the Greek warriors, did not live to see the fall of Troy. He was killed by Paris, who shot an arrow—guided by the god Apollo—into Achilles's only vulnerable spot: his heel. After his death, Achilles's armor was claimed by Odysseus, causing a bitter dispute between Odysseus and Ajax the Great, who felt he deserved the armor. When Odysseus was awarded the armor, Ajax was driven to madness and took his own life.

Aeneas, one of the few Trojan survivors, escaped the destruction of Troy and, according to later Roman mythology, would go on to found the city of Rome, ensuring the continuation of Trojan blood in a new and powerful lineage.

The Trojan War, with its tales of heroism, tragedy, and the whims of the gods, left an indelible mark on Greek culture and mythology. It was a conflict that not only shaped the destinies of its participants but also resonated through the ages, influencing countless works of literature, art, and thought.

CHAPTER 10: THE ODYSSEY

The Odyssey is one of the most celebrated and enduring works of ancient Greek literature, attributed to the poet Homer. Alongside The Iliad, The Odyssey forms a cornerstone of the Greek epic tradition and has had a profound influence on Western literature and culture. While the exact date of its composition is uncertain, it is generally believed to have been written around the 8th century BCE, during the early Archaic period of Greek history.

Homer, traditionally considered the author of both The Iliad and The Odyssey, is a figure shrouded in mystery. Little is known about his life, and some scholars debate whether he was a single individual or a symbolic representation of a collective tradition of oral poets. Regardless of the details of Homer's identity, The Odyssey stands as a masterpiece of epic poetry, recounting the adventures and trials of the hero Odysseus as he struggles to return home after the Trojan War.

Being an entire book in and of itself, I can't share the entire story here. However, if you are interested in reading the entire work, many translations are available online. The following is a condensed version of the Odyssey, detailing the key moments in Odysseus' long journey home after the Trojan war.

***

The Odyssey begins where another great epic, The Iliad, ends—after the fall of Troy. The Trojan War, a decade-long conflict between the Greeks and the city of Troy, has finally ended. The Greeks, led by King Agamemnon, have emerged victorious, largely thanks to the cunning of Odysseus, the king of Ithaca, who devised the strategy of the Trojan Horse, allowing Greek soldiers to infiltrate and destroy the city.

As the war concludes, Odysseus longs to return to his homeland, Ithaca, where his wife, Penelope, and his young son, Telemachus, await him. However, Odysseus's journey home will not be easy. The gods, angered by the hubris of the Greeks and particularly by certain actions of Odysseus, are determined to make his voyage a perilous and prolonged one. What should have been a straightforward journey turns into a ten-year odyssey filled with trials, tribulations, and adventures.

Odysseus's fleet sets sail from Troy, but they are soon blown off course by a storm sent by the god Poseidon, who bears a personal grudge against Odysseus. The fleet lands on the island of the Lotus-Eaters, a people who consume a fruit that causes them to forget their homes and lose all desire to return. Some of Odysseus's men eat the lotus fruit and fall into a stupor, but Odysseus, recognizing the danger, forces them back to the ships and sails away, determined to continue their journey home.

Their next stop brings them to the island of the Cyclopes, a race of one-eyed giants. Odysseus and his men venture into the cave of one of these giants, Polyphemus, who is a son of Poseidon. Polyphemus traps them inside his cave and begins to eat them one by one. Odysseus, ever resourceful, devises a plan to escape. He offers Polyphemus wine and tells him that his name is "Nobody." When the giant falls into a drunken sleep, Odysseus and his men drive a sharpened stake into Polyphemus's single eye, blinding him. As Polyphemus cries out in pain, he calls for help from the other Cyclopes, but when they ask who is hurting him, he replies, "Nobody," leading them to think that he is unharmed.

The next morning, Odysseus and his men escape by clinging to the undersides of Polyphemus's sheep as they are let out to graze. Once safely aboard their ships, Odysseus, in a moment of pride, reveals his true name to Polyphemus, who then prays to his father, Poseidon, to curse Odysseus's journey. Poseidon, angered by Odysseus's arrogance, vows to make his journey home as difficult as possible.

After their narrow escape from the Cyclopes, Odysseus and his men arrive at the island of Aeolus, the god of the winds. Aeolus, recognizing Odysseus's valor, gifts him a bag containing all the winds, except the west wind, which will carry them safely home to Ithaca. For nine days and nights, the fleet sails peacefully, guided by the favorable west wind. However, as they near Ithaca, Odysseus's men, curious about the contents of the bag, open it while Odysseus sleeps. The winds are released, and a violent storm blows the ships off course, sending them back to Aeolus's island.

When they return, Aeolus, believing that Odysseus is cursed by the gods, refuses to help them again, and they are forced to continue their journey on their own. Their next stop is the land of the Laestrygonians, a race of giant cannibals. The Laestrygonians attack the fleet, destroying all the ships except for Odysseus's, which escapes with a small number of survivors.

Odysseus and his remaining men then arrive on the island of Aeaea, home to the sorceress Circe. Circe, a powerful enchantress, lures some of Odysseus's men into her palace with a feast and then uses her magic to turn them into pigs. When Odysseus learns of this, he sets out to rescue his men. Along the way, he is met by the god Hermes, who gives him a magical herb called moly, which will protect him from Circe's spells.

Armed with the moly, Odysseus confronts Circe, and when her magic fails to work on him, she is impressed by his resistance and agrees to turn his men back into their human forms. Odysseus and his men remain on Aeaea for a year, enjoying Circe's hospitality, before they are reminded of their need to return home. Circe, now an ally, advises Odysseus to seek the wisdom of the blind prophet Tiresias in the Underworld, who can guide him on the rest of his journey.

Following Circe's instructions, Odysseus and his men sail to the entrance of the Underworld, a place where no living man had ever ventured. There, Odysseus performs the necessary rituals to summon the spirits of the dead. The first to appear is the spirit of Elpenor, one of Odysseus's men who had died on Aeaea and was left unburied. Elpenor begs Odysseus to return to Aeaea to give him a proper burial, and Odysseus promises to do so.

Next, Odysseus encounters the spirit of Tiresias, who reveals that Poseidon's wrath will continue to haunt him, but that he can still reach Ithaca if he avoids harming the cattle of the sun god, Helios. Tiresias also warns him of the troubles awaiting him at home, including the suitors vying for Penelope's hand in marriage.

Odysseus then speaks with the spirit of his mother, Anticlea, who informs him of the suffering of Penelope and Telemachus in his absence. He also meets the spirits of many famous heroes, including Agamemnon, Achilles, and Ajax, who share their own tales of woe and offer advice.

After his journey to the Underworld, Odysseus and his men return to Aeaea to bury Elpenor. Circe provides them with further guidance on the perils that lie ahead, including the Sirens, Scylla, and Charybdis.

As they set sail once again, Odysseus and his men approach the island of the Sirens, dangerous creatures whose enchanting songs lure sailors to their deaths. Remembering Circe's advice, Odysseus orders his men to plug their ears with beeswax so they cannot hear the Sirens' song. He, however, curious to hear their voices, has himself tied to the mast of the ship and orders his men not to release him, no matter how much he begs.

As they sail past the Sirens, their hauntingly beautiful voices fill the air, and Odysseus is overcome with a desperate longing to go to them. He struggles against his bonds and pleads with his men to release him, but they follow his orders and keep him tied to the mast until they are safely out of earshot.

Next, they must navigate the strait between Scylla and Charybdis, two deadly monsters. Scylla is a six-headed creature that devours sailors from passing ships, while Charybdis is a massive whirlpool that swallows entire vessels. Circe had warned Odysseus that it was better to face Scylla and lose a few men than to risk losing the entire ship to Charybdis.

Following her advice, Odysseus steers the ship close to Scylla's lair. As they pass, Scylla strikes, snatching six of Odysseus's men with her six heads. The rest of the crew sails on, mourning the loss of their comrades but thankful to have survived the encounter.

After their harrowing escape from Scylla and Charybdis, Odysseus and his men reach the island of Thrinacia, where the sacred cattle of the sun god, Helios, graze. Remembering Tiresias's warning, Odysseus instructs his men not to harm the cattle, no matter how hungry they become. However, a fierce storm forces them to remain on the island for an extended period, and as their provisions run out, the men grow desperate.

While Odysseus is away praying to the gods, his men, led by Eurylochus, slaughter the cattle of Helios and feast on them. When Odysseus returns and discovers what they have done, he is filled with dread, knowing that their disobedience will bring dire consequences.

Helios, enraged by the sacrilege, demands that Zeus punish the men. Zeus obliges and sends a violent storm that destroys their ship. All of Odysseus's men perish in the sea, and only Odysseus survives, clinging to a piece of the wreckage.

Odysseus drifts at sea for many days until he is washed ashore on the island of Ogygia, home to the beautiful nymph Calypso. Calypso rescues Odysseus and falls in love with him, offering him immortality if he will stay with her as her husband. Although Odysseus is tempted by her offer, his longing to return home to Ithaca and to Penelope never wavers.

For seven years, Odysseus remains on Ogygia, unable to leave because Calypso will not allow it. However, the gods, particularly Athena, take pity on him. Athena appeals to Zeus, who sends Hermes to Ogygia with a command for Calypso to release Odysseus. Reluctantly, Calypso agrees, helping Odysseus build a raft so he can continue his journey.

Odysseus sets sail once more, but Poseidon, still angry, sends another storm that wrecks his raft. Exhausted and nearly drowned, Odysseus washes ashore on the island of the Phaeacians, where he is discovered by the princess Nausicaa. She takes him to the palace of her father, King Alcinous, where Odysseus is treated with great hospitality.

During a banquet in his honor, Odysseus recounts the story of his long journey, from the end of the Trojan War to his arrival on the shores of the Phaeacians. Moved by his tale, King Alcinous agrees to help him return to Ithaca. The Phaeacians provide Odysseus with a ship, and they safely escort him back to his homeland.

After ten years of war and another 10 years of wandering, Odysseus finally returns to Ithaca. However, his homecoming is not without challenges. During his absence, a group of arrogant suitors has taken over his palace, vying for Penelope's hand in marriage and devouring his wealth. Penelope, faithful to Odysseus, has delayed choosing a new husband by weaving and unweaving a shroud, claiming she will make her decision when the shroud is finished.

Odysseus arrives in Ithaca disguised as a beggar, thanks to the help of Athena, who guides and protects him. He first visits the loyal swineherd, Eumaeus, who does not recognize his master but treats him kindly. Odysseus then reunites with his son, Telemachus, who has grown into a young man during his father's absence. Together, they plot to defeat the suitors and reclaim the palace.

Before revealing himself, Odysseus tests the loyalty of those in his household. Penelope, still mourning her missing husband, devises a contest to choose her new husband: whoever can string Odysseus's great bow and shoot an arrow through twelve axeheads will win her hand. None of the suitors can complete the task, but the disguised Odysseus steps forward and effortlessly strings the bow, firing the arrow through the axeheads.

At that moment, Odysseus throws off his disguise, revealing his true identity. With the help of Telemachus, Eumaeus, and a few loyal servants, Odysseus slays the suitors, reclaiming his home and his throne.

After the suitors are defeated, Penelope is cautious, unsure if the man before her is truly her long-lost husband. To test him, she orders her servant to move their marriage bed, a task she knows is impossible because the bed is built into an olive tree. When Odysseus reacts with indignation, knowing the bed cannot be moved, Penelope realizes that this man is indeed her husband. Overcome with joy, she embraces Odysseus, and they are finally reunited after twenty long years.

Peace is restored in Ithaca, but there is still one more challenge for Odysseus to face. The families of the slain suitors seek revenge, but Athena intervenes, bringing about a truce. Odysseus's journey is finally at an end, and he can now enjoy a peaceful life with his family.

CHAPTER 11: THESEUS AND THE MINOTAUR

Long ago, in the city of Athens, a terrible curse had befallen the people. This curse was the result of a conflict between Athens and the powerful island kingdom of Crete, ruled by King Minos. The origins of this curse can be traced back to a tragic event involving Minos's son, Androgeus.

Androgeus, a skilled and valiant warrior, had traveled to Athens to participate in the Panathenaic Games, a festival held in honor of the goddess Athena. During the games, Androgeus's strength and skill won him many victories, but his success also sparked jealousy and anger among the Athenians. In a fit of envy and fear, some of the Athenian nobles plotted against Androgeus and treacherously ambushed him, leading to his death.

When King Minos learned of his son's death, he was consumed by grief and rage. He vowed to take revenge on Athens for the murder of Androgeus. Minos declared war on Athens, and with the might of his naval forces, he besieged the city. The Athenians, realizing they were no match for the power of Crete, sought to negotiate a truce.

Minos agreed to spare Athens, but only under one cruel condition: every nine years, the Athenians would be required to send seven young men and seven young women to Crete as tribute. These youths would be sent into the labyrinth—a vast, complex maze designed by the legendary architect Daedalus—and there, they would face the Minotaur, a monstrous creature that dwelled within the labyrinth's twisting passages. The Minotaur, a fearsome beast with the body of a man and the head of a bull, was the offspring of Minos's wife, Pasiphaë, and a majestic bull sent by the god Poseidon.

The Athenians, stricken with fear and despair, had no choice but to agree to Minos's demands. For many years, the tragic ritual continued, with the youth of Athens being sacrificed to the Minotaur, never to return. The people of Athens lived in constant sorrow, mourning the loss of their children and dreading the next time they would have to send more to their doom.

As the third cycle of tribute approached, a young hero named Theseus stepped forward to end the suffering of his people. Theseus was the son of Aegeus, the king of Athens, and Aethra, a princess of Troezen. From a young age, Theseus had been raised to be strong, courageous, and virtuous, and he had already proven his heroism through a series of dangerous exploits. When he learned of the fate that awaited the youth of Athens, Theseus could not stand by and allow the horror to continue.

Determined to put an end to the curse, Theseus volunteered to be one of the fourteen tributes sent to Crete. He assured his father, King Aegeus, that he would kill the Minotaur and return victorious. Before he departed, Theseus and Aegeus agreed on a signal: if Theseus was successful, he would return to Athens with white sails on his ship; if he failed, the ship would bear black sails, signaling his death.

With this promise, Theseus set sail for Crete with the other tributes. The journey was long and filled with uncertainty, but Theseus's resolve never wavered. He knew that he had the strength and cunning to defeat the Minotaur, and he was determined to save not only himself and his fellow tributes, but also the future generations of Athens.

When Theseus and the other Athenian youths arrived in Crete, they were taken to
the palace of King Minos, where they were treated as prisoners awaiting their grim
fate. The people of Crete looked upon them with a mix of pity and contempt,
knowing that they were destined to be devoured by the Minotaur.

However, unbeknownst to King Minos, his daughter Ariadne had taken an interest in the young Athenian prince. Ariadne, who was known for her beauty and
intelligence, was moved by Theseus's bravery and determination. She resolved
to help him, for she could not bear the thought of such a noble hero meeting a
gruesome end.

On the eve of Theseus's entry into the labyrinth, Ariadne secretly approached
him and offered her assistance. She provided him with a ball of thread, known as
a "clew," and instructed him to tie one end to the entrance of the labyrinth. As he
ventured into the maze, he would unwind the thread, leaving a trail that would
allow him to find his way back after facing the Minotaur.

Ariadne's guidance gave Theseus hope. With the clew in hand, he entered the
labyrinth, determined to find and slay the Minotaur. The labyrinth was a vast and
bewildering structure, designed to confuse and disorient anyone who entered.
The walls were high, the passages twisted and turned in every direction, and there
was no light to guide his way.

As Theseus ventured deeper into the labyrinth, the air grew thick with the scent of
damp stone and the sound of distant echoes. The darkness pressed in around him,
and he could hear the faint, menacing growls of the Minotaur, hidden somewhere
in the maze. Despite the fear that gripped his heart, Theseus pressed on, his hand
firmly gripping the sword he had brought with him.

Finally, after what seemed like an eternity of wandering through the maze, Theseus came upon the lair of the Minotaur. The beast was even more terrifying
than he had imagined. It stood tall and menacing, with powerful muscles rippling
beneath its coarse fur and eyes that glowed with a savage hunger. The Minotaur

roared, its voice echoing through the labyrinth, and charged at Theseus with ferocious speed.

But Theseus was ready. He deftly dodged the Minotaur's initial attack, using his agility and quick reflexes to stay out of reach of the beast's deadly horns. The two engaged in a fierce battle, with the Minotaur using its brute strength and Theseus relying on his speed and cunning. The narrow confines of the labyrinth made the fight even more dangerous, as both combatants had little room to maneuver.

The battle raged on, with Theseus narrowly avoiding the Minotaur's powerful strikes. The beast's rage grew with every missed blow, and Theseus knew that he could not afford to let his guard down for even a moment. Finally, after a grueling struggle, Theseus saw an opening. Summoning all his strength, he delivered a powerful strike to the Minotaur's neck, driving his sword deep into the creature's flesh.

The Minotaur let out a final, agonized roar as it collapsed to the ground, its lifeblood staining the cold stone of the labyrinth. Theseus stood over the fallen beast, his chest heaving with exhaustion, but his heart filled with triumph. He had done what no one else had been able to do—he had slain the Minotaur.

With the Minotaur defeated, Theseus quickly retraced his steps using the thread that Ariadne had given him. He wound his way back through the labyrinth, following the trail until he reached the entrance. When he emerged from the maze, the other Athenian youths, who had been waiting in fear and uncertainty, greeted him with astonishment and joy. They could hardly believe that Theseus had succeeded in his perilous mission.

Ariadne, who had anxiously awaited Theseus's return, was overjoyed to see him emerge from the labyrinth alive. She had risked everything to help him, and now that he had triumphed, she knew that she could not remain in Crete. Ariadne asked Theseus to take her with him back to Athens, and he agreed. Together, they and the other Athenian youths fled the palace under the cover of night, making their way to the ship that had brought them to Crete.

The journey back to Athens was filled with a sense of relief and celebration. The Athenian youths, once destined to be sacrificed to the Minotaur, now sailed home as heroes. Theseus had not only saved their lives, but he had also freed Athens from the terrible tribute that had plagued the city for so many years.

However, the journey also brought with it a tragic turn of events. During the voyage, the ship stopped at the island of Naxos. While there, Theseus had a dream in which the god Dionysus appeared to him and demanded that he leave Ariadne on the island, for she was destined to become the god's bride. When Theseus awoke, he reluctantly complied with the god's command, leaving Ariadne behind as the ship set sail for Athens.

As the ship neared Athens, Theseus was filled with anticipation at the thought of reuniting with his father, King Aegeus. He had fulfilled his promise and defeated the Minotaur, bringing an end to the curse that had haunted Athens. However, in the excitement of the journey, Theseus forgot to change the ship's sails from black to white, as he had agreed with his father.

King Aegeus had been anxiously watching the horizon for his son's return, and when he saw the ship approaching with its black sails, he believed that Theseus had perished in Crete. Overcome with grief, Aegeus threw himself from the cliffs into the sea, ending his life. The sea where he fell would forever bear his name—the Aegean Sea. When Theseus finally arrived in Athens and learned of his father's tragic death, he was devastated. The joy of his victory over the Minotaur was overshadowed by the loss of his father, a loss that he unintentionally caused.

Despite this sorrow, Theseus was welcomed back to Athens as a hero. The people of Athens celebrated his return and his triumph over the Minotaur, and Theseus was hailed as the savior of the city. With Aegeus gone, Theseus ascended to the throne, becoming the new king of Athens. He dedicated himself to ruling with wisdom and justice, determined to honor his father's memory and to protect the city that had placed its trust in him.

CHAPTER 12: JASON AND THE ARGONAUTS

The story of Jason and the Argonauts begins with a tale of betrayal and rightful vengeance in the kingdom of Iolcus in Thessaly. The rightful king of Iolcus, Aeson, was overthrown by his half-brother, Pelias, who seized the throne for himself. Fearing for his life, Aeson sent his infant son, Jason, away to be raised in secret by the wise centaur Chiron. Under Chiron's care, Jason grew into a strong and courageous young man, unaware of his true lineage. However, when he came of age, Jason learned of his royal heritage and his father's unjust overthrow. Determined to reclaim his rightful throne, Jason set out for Iolcus to confront Pelias.

As Jason approached Iolcus, he encountered an old woman struggling to cross a river. Despite the difficulty, Jason carried her across, unaware that the woman was actually the goddess Hera in disguise. Grateful for his kindness, Hera decided to aid Jason in his quest, though she also saw it as an opportunity to punish Pelias, who had offended her in the past. When Jason arrived in Iolcus, he confronted Pelias and demanded the throne. Pelias, recognizing Jason as a threat, devised a cunning plan to rid himself of the young hero. He agreed to relinquish the throne, but only if Jason could accomplish an impossible task: retrieving the Golden Fleece, a legendary artifact said to possess magical powers and guarded by a fearsome dragon in the distant land of Colchis.

The Golden Fleece was no ordinary treasure. It was the fleece of a divine ram that had once saved Phrixus, the son of a Boeotian king, from being sacrificed. The ram had carried Phrixus to safety in Colchis, a kingdom located on the eastern shores of the Black Sea. In gratitude, Phrixus sacrificed the ram to Zeus and presented its golden fleece to King Aeëtes of Colchis, who hung it in a sacred grove guarded by a sleepless dragon. Despite the dangers, Jason accepted Pelias's challenge, knowing that success would restore his father's throne and bring him glory. However, the journey to Colchis was fraught with peril, and Jason knew he could not undertake it alone. He called upon the greatest heroes of Greece to join him on his quest, forming a legendary crew known as the Argonauts, named after their ship, the Argo.

The Argonauts were a group of the most formidable and renowned heroes of the age, including Heracles, the strongest of all mortals and a son of Zeus; Orpheus, the master musician whose songs could charm even the rocks and trees; Castor and Pollux, twin brothers known for their martial prowess and horsemanship; Atalanta, the swift-footed huntress who could outrun any man; Meleager, the hero who would later hunt the Calydonian Boar; Peleus, the father of Achilles, and Telamon, the father of Ajax, both skilled warriors; and Argus, the builder of the Argo, whose ship was blessed by the gods. With this mighty crew assembled, Jason prepared to set sail.

The journey of the Argonauts was filled with challenges and adventures as they sailed through treacherous waters and encountered both mortal and divine obstacles. The first stop on their voyage was the Isle of Lemnos, inhabited solely by women. The women of Lemnos, led by their queen Hypsipyle, had killed their husbands and male kin in a fit of rage, and they now lived alone. The Argonauts were welcomed with open arms, and Jason himself formed a relationship with Hypsipyle. The crew remained on Lemnos for some time, but eventually, they resumed their journey, with Jason reminding them of their mission.

The Argonauts next arrived in the land of the Doliones, ruled by King Cyzicus. They were warmly received by the king, but their departure was marred by a tragic misunderstanding. During the night, a storm blew the Argo back to the shores of Doliones, and in the darkness, the Doliones mistook the Argonauts for enemies and attacked them. In the ensuing battle, Jason killed King Cyzicus, only realizing the tragic mistake when daylight revealed the truth. The Argonauts mourned the king and held funeral games in his honor before continuing their journey.

As they sailed onward, the Argonauts encountered the river Cius, where Heracles's squire, Hylas, was abducted by water nymphs who fell in love with his beauty. Heracles, devastated by the loss of his beloved companion, searched for Hylas but was unable to find him. The Argonauts, pressed for time, were forced to leave Heracles behind as they continued their voyage, marking a significant loss for the crew. The Argonauts then reached the land of Thrace, where they found the blind seer Phineus, tormented by the Harpies—vicious creatures who stole or befouled his food whenever he tried to eat. The Argonauts, with the help of the Boreads (the winged sons of Boreas, the North Wind), drove off the Harpies, freeing Phineus from his torment. In return, Phineus gave Jason crucial advice on how to navigate the Symplegades, the Clashing Rocks that guarded the entrance to the Black Sea.

The Symplegades were two massive rocks that crashed together, crushing any ship that attempted to pass between them. Following Phineus's advice, the Argonauts released a dove to fly through the rocks first. The dove made it through with only its tail feathers clipped, signaling that the Argonauts could follow. As the Argo passed between the rocks, the crew rowed with all their might, and with the help of Athena, they narrowly escaped being crushed. Once they had passed, the rocks became fixed in place, allowing future sailors to pass safely.

After many adventures, the Argonauts finally reached Colchis, where the Golden Fleece was guarded by King Aeëtes. Aeëtes was a powerful and cunning ruler, and he had no intention of giving up the Golden Fleece. He challenged Jason to complete a series of impossible tasks in exchange for the fleece, fully expecting the hero to fail and perish in the attempt. The first task was to yoke two fire-breathing bulls with bronze hooves and use them to plow a field sacred to the war god Ares.

The second task was to sow the field with dragon's teeth, from which an army of warriors would spring up, ready to fight. The third task was to defeat these warriors and survive the onslaught.

Desperate for help, Jason sought the aid of Medea, the daughter of King Aeëtes, who was a powerful sorceress. Medea had fallen in love with Jason, either through divine intervention by Hera and Aphrodite or by her own will, depending on the version of the myth. She agreed to help him, but only if he promised to take her with him and make her his wife. Medea provided Jason with a magical ointment that made him invulnerable to fire and weapons for a day. With this protection, Jason was able to yoke the bulls and plow the field. Following Medea's instructions, he then sowed the dragon's teeth and, as the warriors sprang from the earth, he threw a rock among them. The warriors, confused and unable to determine where the rock had come from, turned on each other and fought until they were all slain.

Despite completing the tasks, Aeëtes still refused to give up the Golden Fleece. Medea, realizing her father's treachery, led Jason to the sacred grove where the fleece was kept, guarded by a sleepless dragon. Using her magic, Medea lulled the dragon to sleep, allowing Jason to seize the Golden Fleece. With the fleece in hand, Jason and Medea fled Colchis, pursued by Aeëtes and his forces. To delay her father, Medea killed her own brother, Apsyrtus, and scattered his dismembered body into the sea. Aeëtes, grief-stricken, halted his pursuit to collect his son's remains, giving the Argonauts the time they needed to escape.

The journey back to Iolcus was fraught with challenges, as the Argonauts faced the wrath of the gods and the consequences of their actions in Colchis. After fleeing Colchis, Jason and Medea sought purification for the murder of Apsyrtus. They arrived on the island of Aeaea, where the sorceress Circe, Medea's aunt, lived. Circe performed the necessary rites to cleanse them of their sin, but she also warned them that the gods would not overlook their actions so easily. The Argonauts next encountered the Sirens, dangerous creatures whose enchanting songs lured sailors to their doom. Forewarned by Circe, the Argonauts had Orpheus play his lyre and sing more beautifully than the Sirens, drowning out their voices and allowing the ship to pass safely. The Argonauts then faced a series of maritime perils, including the monstrous Scylla, the whirlpool Charybdis, and the Wandering Rocks. With the guidance of the sea nymph Thetis and her sisters, the Nereids, they managed to navigate these dangers and continue their journey.

The Argonauts sought refuge on the island of the Phaeacians, ruled by King Alcinous and Queen Arete. Here, the Colchian fleet caught up with them, demanding that Medea be returned. However, Queen Arete intervened and ensured that Jason and Medea were married, securing Medea's protection under the laws of hospitality. As they neared Crete, the Argonauts encountered Talos, a giant bronze automaton who guarded the island. Talos attempted to prevent the Argonauts from landing, but Medea used her magic to exploit his one weakness—a single vein running from his neck to his ankle that was sealed with a nail. She removed the nail, causing Talos to bleed out and collapse.

Upon their return to Iolcus, Jason presented the Golden Fleece to Pelias, expecting to reclaim the throne. However, Pelias refused to relinquish power, prompting Medea to take matters into her own hands. She devised a cunning and ruthless plan to overthrow Pelias. Medea convinced the daughters of Pelias that she could restore their father's youth by cutting him into pieces and boiling him in a cauldron with magical herbs. To prove her claim, she demonstrated the process on an old ram, transforming it into a young lamb. Eager to rejuvenate their father, the daughters followed Medea's instructions, but Medea deliberately withheld the magical herbs, leaving Pelias dead and dismembered.

The murder of Pelias, however, did not lead to Jason's ascension to the throne. Instead, Pelias's son, Acastus, drove Jason and Medea into exile. They fled to Corinth, where they lived for several years and had children. In Corinth, the story takes a darker turn. Jason, driven by ambition, sought to marry Glauce, the daughter of King Creon, in order to secure power and position. Feeling betrayed, Medea exacted a terrible revenge. She sent Glauce a poisoned robe, which burned her to death when she put it on. In a final act of vengeance, Medea killed her own children by Jason to deprive him of any legacy. She then fled to Athens in a chariot provided by her grandfather, the sun god Helios. Jason, devastated and alone, lost everything he had fought for. According to some versions of the myth, he died a broken man, struck down by a piece of the Argo's rotting timber as he sat beside the beached ship, a tragic end for the once-great hero.

CHAPTER 13: THE TRAGEDY OF OEDIPUS

In the ancient city of Thebes, a prophecy loomed over the royal family—a prophecy that would lead to one of the most tragic and well-known tales in Greek mythology. Laius, the king of Thebes, and his wife, Queen Jocasta, were troubled by an oracle's prophecy that foretold a terrible fate: their son, when born, would grow up to kill his father and marry his mother, bringing ruin to their house.

The prophecy filled Laius and Jocasta with fear and dread. Desperate to prevent the prophecy from coming true, Laius took drastic measures. When their son was born, Laius ordered that the infant be taken to the mountains and left to die. To ensure that the child could not crawl away, Laius had the baby's ankles pierced and bound together. The child was then handed over to a loyal servant, who was instructed to abandon him on Mount Cithaeron.

However, the servant could not bring himself to leave the helpless infant to die. Instead, he handed the baby over to a shepherd from the nearby kingdom of Corinth. The shepherd, moved by pity, decided to take the child to the king and queen of Corinth, who were childless and longing for an heir.

King Polybus and Queen Merope of Corinth were overjoyed to receive the child, whom they named Oedipus, meaning "swollen foot" in reference to the injury to his ankles. They raised Oedipus as their own son, never revealing the secret of his true parentage. Oedipus grew up believing he was the legitimate heir to the throne of Corinth, unaware of the dark fate that awaited him.

As Oedipus reached manhood, he began to hear rumors questioning his parentage. Troubled by these whispers, he sought out the Oracle of Delphi, the most revered source of prophecy in the ancient world, to learn the truth about his origins. The oracle, however, did not answer his question directly. Instead, she delivered a chilling prophecy of her own: Oedipus was destined to kill his father and marry his mother.

Horrified by this revelation, Oedipus resolved to flee Corinth, believing that by doing so, he could escape his fate and protect his parents. He left the city and began a journey that would unknowingly lead him closer to the fulfillment of the prophecy.

As Oedipus traveled through the land, he encountered an old man and his entourage on a narrow road. The two parties quarreled over who had the right of way, and in a fit of rage, Oedipus struck down the old man, killing him and several of his attendants. Unbeknownst to Oedipus, the old man was none other than King Laius, his biological father. In this moment of violence, Oedipus had unknowingly taken the first step toward fulfilling the prophecy.

After the confrontation on the road, Oedipus continued his journey and eventually arrived at the city of Thebes. The city was in turmoil, terrorized by a monstrous creature known as the Sphinx. The Sphinx was a fearsome beast with the body of a lion, the wings of an eagle, and the head of a woman. She had taken up residence near Thebes and would challenge all who approached with a riddle. Those who failed to answer correctly were devoured by the Sphinx.

The riddle posed by the Sphinx was as follows: "What walks on four legs in the morning, two legs at noon, and three legs in the evening?" Many had tried to solve the riddle and failed, meeting a gruesome end. Thebes was in despair, and the people were desperate for a hero who could rid them of this menace.

When Oedipus arrived in Thebes, he was confronted by the Sphinx and challenged to answer the riddle. With his sharp mind and quick wit, Oedipus solved the riddle, answering, "Man." He explained that a man crawls on all fours as a baby, walks on two legs as an adult, and uses a cane in old age, thus walking on three legs.

The Sphinx, defeated by Oedipus's correct answer, threw herself off a cliff, freeing Thebes from her terror. The people of Thebes hailed Oedipus as a hero, and in gratitude, they offered him the throne of Thebes, as their king had recently been killed by an unknown assailant. Additionally, Oedipus was given the hand of the widowed Queen Jocasta in marriage. Oedipus, unaware of the true identity of either Jocasta or the man he had killed on the road, accepted both the throne and the queen, thus unknowingly fulfilling the second part of the prophecy.

Years passed, and under Oedipus's rule, Thebes prospered. He and Jocasta had four children together—two sons, Eteocles and Polynices, and two daughters, Antigone and Ismene. The people of Thebes respected and admired their king, who had brought them peace and prosperity.

However, Thebes was struck by a terrible plague. Crops failed, livestock died, and the people were ravaged by sickness. The city was plunged into despair, and the citizens turned to Oedipus for help, begging him to save them from this calamity.

Determined to find a solution, Oedipus sent Creon, his brother-in-law, to the Oracle of Delphi to seek guidance. When Creon returned, he brought a message from the oracle: the plague was a punishment for the unavenged murder of King Laius, the former king of Thebes. The murderer was still living in Thebes, and until he was found and brought to justice, the city would continue to suffer.

Oedipus, unaware that he himself was the murderer, vowed to find the culprit and bring him to justice. He declared that the killer would be banished from Thebes, and he called upon the people to come forward with any information they might have.

As Oedipus began his investigation, he sought the help of the blind prophet Tiresias, who was known for his wisdom and insight. Tiresias was reluctant to reveal what he knew, but when pressed by Oedipus, he finally spoke the truth: Oedipus himself was the murderer of King Laius, and the prophecy had been fulfilled—he had killed his father and married his mother.

Oedipus, furious at what he believed to be a lie, accused Tiresias of conspiring against him. He refused to accept the prophet's words and continued his search for the truth. However, as the investigation progressed, more and more pieces of the puzzle began to fall into place.

A messenger from Corinth arrived with news that King Polybus, Oedipus's adoptive father, had died of natural causes. This seemed to contradict the prophecy, but the messenger also revealed that Oedipus was not the biological son of Polybus and Merope. The messenger, who had been the shepherd who found the infant Oedipus on Mount Cithaeron, recounted how he had delivered the baby to the king and queen of Corinth.

This revelation led Oedipus to question the servant who had been ordered to abandon him as a child. The servant, now an old man, confirmed the terrible truth: Oedipus was the son of Laius and Jocasta, and the prophecy had come true. Oedipus had killed his father on the road to Thebes and had married his mother, bringing about the very fate that he had tried so desperately to avoid.

When Jocasta realized the truth, she was overwhelmed with horror and despair. Unable to bear the shame and guilt of her actions, she fled to the palace and hanged herself. Oedipus, upon discovering Jocasta's body, was consumed by grief and self-loathing. In a fit of anguish, he took the brooches from her dress and used them to gouge out his own eyes, blinding himself as punishment for his sins.

Blinded and broken, Oedipus relinquished the throne of Thebes. He begged to be exiled from the city, believing that only in banishment could he atone for the suffering he had caused. Creon, now the ruler of Thebes, granted Oedipus's request and allowed him to leave the city.

Accompanied by his daughter Antigone, who remained loyal to him despite his fall from grace, Oedipus wandered the land as a blind and destitute exile. His once-great life had been reduced to nothing, and he was left to grapple with the weight of his actions and the inescapable nature of fate.

As Oedipus neared the end of his life, he received a vision that revealed the location where he would die. He asked Theseus to take him to the sacred grove of the Eumenides, also known as the Furies, who were the goddesses of vengeance and justice. This grove, located in the town of Colonus, was a place of profound spiritual significance, where the boundaries between the mortal world and the divine were thin.

Theseus, understanding the gravity of Oedipus's request, accompanied him to the grove. As they reached the sacred ground, Oedipus felt a deep sense of peace for the first time in many years. He knew that his long journey of suffering and exile was finally coming to an end. Surrounded by the silence and serenity of the grove, Oedipus made his final preparations.

Before he passed, Oedipus made a solemn promise to Theseus: his burial site would bring great blessings to the land of Athens, and the city would forever be protected as long as his grave remained undisturbed. Theseus, moved by Oedipus's tragic fate and the dignity with which he faced his end, promised to honor his request.

In a moment of profound stillness, as the sun began to set, Oedipus was taken by the gods. The exact manner of his death is shrouded in mystery, as it was said that he disappeared into the earth, guided by a divine force. No one, not even Theseus, saw the moment of his passing. The gods, it seemed, had finally shown mercy to Oedipus, taking him away to a place of eternal rest.

Oedipus's daughters, Antigone and Ismene, who had been with him during his final days, mourned the loss of their father but took comfort in the knowledge that his suffering was over. They returned to Thebes, carrying with them the story of their father's tragic life, a tale that would be remembered for generations to come.

CHAPTER 14: THE ABDUCTION OF PERSEPHONE

In the ancient world of Greek mythology, the earth was governed by a cycle of life, death, and rebirth, overseen by a pantheon of gods and goddesses who controlled every aspect of existence. Among these deities was Demeter, the goddess of agriculture, grain, and fertility. Demeter was responsible for the growth of crops and the fertility of the earth, ensuring that humanity had the sustenance it needed to survive. Her power was immense, and her role was vital to the well-being of both gods and mortals.

Demeter had a daughter named Persephone, who was born of her union with Zeus, the king of the gods. Persephone was a beautiful and radiant goddess, embodying the innocence and vitality of youth. She was often depicted as a young maiden adorned with flowers, symbolizing the blossoming of life in the spring. Persephone spent her days in the company of the nymphs, dancing through the meadows, gathering flowers, and enjoying the beauty of the natural world. She was deeply loved by her mother, Demeter, who cherished her daughter above all else.

Persephone's beauty and charm did not go unnoticed by the other gods, and many desired her for a wife. However, Demeter was fiercely protective of her daughter and was reluctant to see her married. She wished to keep Persephone by her side, to share in the joy of her company and to ensure that the earth remained fertile and bountiful through their bond.

Far below the earth, in the dark and shadowy realm of the Underworld, lived Hades, the god of the dead and ruler of the Underworld. Hades was one of the three powerful brothers who divided the cosmos among themselves after the defeat of the Titans—Zeus ruled the heavens, Poseidon the seas, and Hades the Underworld. Though Hades was a powerful god, his realm was one of darkness and isolation, far removed from the light and life of the world above.

Hades rarely ventured out of his gloomy domain, but when he did, he could not help but notice Persephone's beauty. As the god of the dead, Hades had little contact with the joys of life, and Persephone's vibrant energy captivated him. He longed to have her as his queen, to bring a touch of life and light into his dark kingdom. However, Hades knew that Demeter would never willingly allow her daughter to join him in the Underworld, so he devised a plan to take Persephone by force.

Hades sought the counsel of his brother Zeus, knowing that the king of the gods held great influence over the fates of both gods and mortals. Zeus, though he loved his daughter, was not as protective as Demeter, and he recognized the value of such a union. Hades proposed to Zeus that he would abduct Persephone and take her to the Underworld as his bride, and Zeus, after some consideration, agreed. He gave Hades his consent, though he warned him that Demeter would not take the loss of her daughter lightly.

With Zeus's permission, Hades prepared to carry out his plan. He knew that he would need to act swiftly and decisively, for once Persephone was in the Underworld, there would be little that Demeter could do to retrieve her.

One bright day, as the sun shone warmly over the earth, Persephone was wandering through the fields, accompanied by her nymph companions. The meadows were alive with the colors of spring, and Persephone delighted in the abundance of flowers that surrounded her. She moved from one blossom to the next, filling her arms with fragrant blooms, her laughter ringing through the air.

As she gathered flowers, Persephone came upon a particularly enchanting bloom—a narcissus, which had been planted there by Gaia, the earth goddess, at the request of Zeus to lure Persephone. The flower was unlike any she had ever seen, with its petals glowing like gold and its fragrance intoxicating. Drawn to its beauty, Persephone reached out to pluck the flower from the earth.

At that moment, the ground beneath her feet began to tremble, and a deep chasm opened in the earth. Before Persephone could react, Hades emerged from the underworld in his chariot drawn by four black horses. In a flash, he seized Persephone and carried her off, descending back into the chasm, which closed behind them, leaving no trace of the abduction.

The nymphs who had been with Persephone were stunned and terrified, unable to comprehend what had just occurred. They searched frantically for their mistress, calling out her name, but she was nowhere to be found. The earth was silent, and the meadows, once filled with laughter and song, were now eerily quiet. The nymphs, unable to find Persephone, wept bitterly and eventually fled, fearing Demeter's wrath.

When Demeter learned of her daughter's disappearance, she was overcome with grief and panic. She searched the earth tirelessly, calling out for Persephone, but received no answer. The once bountiful and fertile land began to wither as Demeter's sorrow deepened, and the crops that had flourished under her care began to die. The world was plunged into a barren state, and a great famine spread across the land, threatening the lives of both mortals and animals.

For nine days and nights, Demeter wandered the earth, refusing to eat, drink, or rest. She was consumed by her despair, her heart breaking with each passing day that she could not find her beloved daughter. The gods watched from Olympus, concerned by the devastation that Demeter's grief was causing, but none dared to intervene, knowing the depth of her anguish.

On the tenth day, Demeter encountered Hecate, the goddess of witchcraft and the crossroads. Hecate, who had heard Persephone's cries as she was taken, but had not seen the abductor, approached Demeter and offered her sympathy. Together, they went to Helios, the sun god, who sees all that happens in the world from his vantage point in the sky.

Helios, moved by Demeter's sorrow, revealed the truth to her. He told her that it was Hades who had taken Persephone, and that Zeus had given his consent. Upon hearing this, Demeter's sorrow turned to rage. She was furious with Zeus for allowing her daughter to be taken and vowed that she would not allow the earth to bear fruit until Persephone was returned to her.

True to her word, Demeter withdrew her blessings from the earth. The once-fertile land became desolate, and the crops failed to grow. The rivers dried up, the trees shed their leaves, and a harsh winter gripped the world. The people of the earth suffered greatly, and they prayed to the gods for relief, but their pleas went unanswered. Even the gods themselves began to worry, for without the offerings of grain and other produce from the earth, their own existence was threatened.

Zeus, seeing the devastation that Demeter's wrath had caused, realized that he could not allow the situation to continue. The balance of the world was in jeopardy, and the suffering of both mortals and gods had become too great. He knew that he would have to find a way to appease Demeter and bring Persephone back from the Underworld.

Zeus sent Hermes, the messenger of the gods, to the Underworld to speak with Hades and negotiate Persephone's release. Hermes, swift and resourceful, descended to the realm of the dead and found Hades seated on his throne, with Persephone by his side.

When Hermes arrived in the Underworld, he delivered Zeus's message to Hades, explaining the dire situation on earth and the need for Persephone's return. Hades, though reluctant to part with his new bride, understood that he could not defy the will of Zeus and risk the destruction of the world. He agreed to allow Persephone to return to the surface, but not before ensuring that she would not leave him forever.

Before Persephone left the Underworld, Hades offered her a pomegranate, a fruit of the Underworld. Persephone, unaware of the consequences, ate a few seeds from the pomegranate. This act, seemingly innocent, bound her to the Underworld, as it was a rule that anyone who consumed food or drink in the realm of the dead was compelled to return there.

When Hermes brought Persephone back to the surface, Demeter was overjoyed to be reunited with her daughter. The earth began to bloom once more, as Demeter's happiness restored the fertility of the land. The crops grew, the trees regained their leaves, and the people of the earth rejoiced at the return of abundance.

However, their joy was tempered by the revelation that Persephone's time on earth would be limited. Because she had eaten the pomegranate seeds, Persephone was bound to spend part of each year in the Underworld as Hades's queen. For one-third of the year, she would dwell in the Underworld, and during this time, Demeter's grief would cause the earth to wither and die, bringing about the barren season of winter. But for the rest of the year, Persephone would return to the surface, and Demeter's joy would bring about the rebirth of the earth in the spring, followed by the abundance of summer and autumn.

The story of Persephone's abduction and her eventual return to the surface became the mythological explanation for the changing of the seasons. Persephone's descent into the Underworld symbolized the death and dormancy of the earth during the winter months, while her return marked the renewal of life in the spring. The cycle of life, death, and rebirth was embodied in the figure of Persephone, who became the goddess of both the Underworld and the renewal of the earth.

Persephone's dual role as the queen of the Underworld and the bringer of spring made her a complex and powerful figure in Greek mythology. She was both a symbol of life and death, a reminder of the fragility of life and the inevitability of death, but also of the hope and renewal that comes with each new cycle of the seasons.

The story of Persephone and Demeter was also central to the Eleusinian Mysteries, one of the most important religious rites in ancient Greece. These mysteries, held annually in the town of Eleusis, were secret ceremonies that celebrated the themes of life, death, and rebirth, as represented by the myth of Persephone. The participants in the mysteries sought to gain a deeper understanding of the cycle of life and death, as well as a promise of hope and renewal in the afterlife.

The Eleusinian Mysteries were closely guarded, and their rituals were never fully revealed to outsiders. However, it is known that the initiates underwent a series of rites that symbolized the descent into the Underworld and the return to the light, mirroring Persephone's journey. The mysteries were a source of spiritual comfort and enlightenment for those who participated, offering a glimpse of the divine order that governed the cosmos.

CHAPTER 15: ORPHEUS AND EURYDICE

In the ancient world of Thrace, a land known for its rugged beauty and untamed wilderness, there lived a man named Orpheus. He was no ordinary man; Orpheus was the son of the Muse Calliope, the Muse of epic poetry, and the god of music, Apollo. From his divine parentage, Orpheus inherited an extraordinary gift—his music. Orpheus was a master of the lyre, a stringed instrument that he played with such skill and passion that his music could enchant all who heard it.

It was said that when Orpheus played, his music had the power to charm even the most savage of beasts, to make the trees sway in rhythm, and to calm the raging rivers. His voice was as beautiful as his playing, and together, they created melodies so exquisite that gods and mortals alike would stop to listen. Orpheus was renowned throughout the ancient world as the greatest musician who had ever lived.

Orpheus's music was not just a talent; it was a connection to the divine, a reflection of the harmony of the cosmos. His ability to move the hearts of all living creatures made him a beloved figure, respected and admired by all who knew him. But despite the adoration he received, Orpheus was a man of deep emotion, capable of great love and great sorrow.

Among those who were captivated by Orpheus's music was a beautiful young woman named Eurydice. Eurydice was a dryad, a nymph of the trees, and she lived in the forests of Thrace. She was as graceful as she was lovely, and her presence brought life and beauty to the woods she called home. When Orpheus and Eurydice first met, it was love at first sight. The two were drawn to each other, their souls connecting as if they had known each other for eternity.

Orpheus and Eurydice soon became inseparable. Their love blossomed like the flowers in spring, and they spent their days wandering through the forests, Orpheus playing his lyre and singing songs of love for Eurydice. The trees, the animals, and the very earth itself seemed to rejoice in their happiness. It was a love that was pure, untainted by jealousy or fear, and it filled their hearts with joy.

Their love was so strong that they decided to marry, and their wedding was a celebration of their union, attended by nymphs, gods, and mortals alike. The day was filled with music, dancing, and laughter, and the blessings of the gods were upon them. Orpheus and Eurydice believed that they were destined to live a life of eternal happiness, but fate had other plans.

Not long after their wedding, tragedy struck. One day, as Eurydice was walking through the forest, she caught the eye of a shepherd named Aristaeus. Enchanted by her beauty, Aristaeus pursued her with intentions that were far from honorable. Frightened, Eurydice fled, running through the woods as fast as she could. In her haste, she stepped on a serpent hidden in the grass. The snake bit her on the heel, and its venom quickly spread through her body.

Eurydice's scream echoed through the forest, but by the time Orpheus found her, it was too late. The poison had taken its toll, and Eurydice lay lifeless on the ground. Orpheus was devastated. His beloved wife, the light of his life, was gone, and his heart was shattered. He mourned her deeply, his grief so profound that it silenced his music. The world seemed to darken, and all the joy that had once filled his soul was replaced by an overwhelming sorrow.

But Orpheus's love for Eurydice was so strong that he refused to accept her death. He knew that she had been taken to the Underworld, the realm of the dead, ruled by Hades and Persephone. And so, Orpheus made a decision that would change the course of his life—he would go to the Underworld and bring Eurydice back.

Orpheus's journey to the Underworld was one of great peril. No living mortal had ever entered the land of the dead and returned, but Orpheus was determined. He made his way to the entrance of the Underworld, a dark and foreboding cave that led to the River Styx, the boundary between the worlds of the living and the dead. It was here that Charon, the ferryman of the dead, awaited to transport souls across the river.

When Orpheus approached the river, Charon initially refused him passage, for no living soul was permitted to cross. But Orpheus, with his lyre in hand, began to play. The music that flowed from his instrument was so mournful, so filled with longing and love, that it touched even the heart of Charon, who relented and allowed Orpheus to board his boat.

As they crossed the River Styx, the shades of the dead gathered around Orpheus, drawn by the haunting beauty of his music. Even the Furies, the relentless goddesses of vengeance, paused in their eternal pursuit to listen. Orpheus's music reached the very depths of the Underworld, where it moved all who heard it.

When they reached the other side, Orpheus continued his journey, passing through the gates of the Underworld guarded by the monstrous three-headed dog, Cerberus. But even Cerberus, fierce and terrifying as he was, was calmed by Orpheus's song, and he allowed the musician to pass unharmed.

Finally, Orpheus reached the throne room of Hades and Persephone. The king and queen of the Underworld were struck by the mortal's bravery and determination. As Orpheus stood before them, he began to play his lyre and sing a song of such sorrow and love that even the cold heart of Hades was moved.

Orpheus sang of his love for Eurydice, of their happiness together, and of the unbearable grief he felt at her loss. He pleaded with Hades and Persephone to allow Eurydice to return to the world of the living, so that they could be together once more. His music spoke of the power of love, a force so strong that it could defy even death itself.

Hades, who was known for his stern and unyielding nature, was deeply moved by Orpheus's plea. He turned to Persephone, who, as the queen of the Underworld and the goddess of spring, understood the pain of separation from loved ones. Together, they decided to grant Orpheus's request, but with one condition.

Eurydice would be allowed to return to the land of the living, but as they ascended from the Underworld, Orpheus must not look back at her until they had both reached the surface. If he did, even for a moment, Eurydice would be lost to him forever.

Orpheus, filled with hope, agreed to the condition without hesitation. Hades called forth Eurydice, and she appeared before Orpheus, her form ethereal and shadowy, a reflection of her former self. She began to follow Orpheus as he made his way back through the Underworld, with Orpheus leading the way and Eurydice walking behind him.

The journey back to the surface was fraught with tension. Orpheus was filled with both hope and fear—hope that he would soon be reunited with Eurydice, and fear that he might lose her if he succumbed to the temptation to look back. As they ascended the dark and winding path, the silence between them was heavy with the weight of the gods' condition.

Orpheus could hear the soft footsteps of Eurydice behind him, but he could not see her. Doubts began to creep into his mind—was she really there? Was she following him, or had she been left behind? The uncertainty gnawed at him, and the desire to look back and confirm her presence grew stronger with each step.

As they neared the entrance to the Underworld, the light of the surface world began to pierce through the darkness. Orpheus could see the mouth of the cave ahead, and he knew that they were almost free. But just as they were about to emerge into the light, Orpheus's resolve faltered. The fear of losing Eurydice, the love of his life, was too great, and he could not bear the uncertainty any longer.

In a moment of weakness, Orpheus turned to look back at Eurydice. Their eyes met for a brief, heart-wrenching moment, and Orpheus saw the love and sorrow in her gaze. But as soon as he looked back, the bond between them was broken. Eurydice began to fade away, her form dissolving into the shadows of the Underworld. She reached out to Orpheus, but it was too late. She was pulled back into the depths, her final words a faint echo of his name.

Orpheus, overcome with despair, tried to follow her, but the gates of the Underworld closed before him. He was left alone at the entrance, his heart shattered and his love lost forever.

The loss of Eurydice was a blow from which Orpheus would never recover. He wandered the earth in mourning, his music now filled with sorrow and lamentation. The joy that had once defined his melodies was gone, replaced by a haunting sadness that echoed through the forests and valleys of Thrace. Orpheus no longer took pleasure in the things he once loved, and he withdrew from the world, lost in his grief.

Orpheus's story did not have a happy ending. According to some versions of the myth, he was eventually killed by the Maenads, the frenzied followers of Dionysus, who were angered by his refusal to honor their god. They tore him apart, and his head and lyre were thrown into the River Hebrus, where they continued to sing mournful songs as they floated downstream.

CHAPTER 16: ECHO AND NARCISSUS

In the lush, verdant forests of ancient Greece, there lived a beautiful nymph named Echo. Like all nymphs, Echo was a creature of nature, embodying the beauty and charm of the wild landscapes she inhabited. She was one of the Oreads, the nymphs of the mountains, and her days were spent flitting through the trees, dancing beside streams, and singing with her melodious voice that could enchant all who heard it.

Echo was not only beautiful but also exceptionally talkative. She loved engaging in conversation and was known for her witty and pleasant discourse. However, this love of chatter would soon lead her into trouble. Zeus, the king of the gods, was known for his many amorous adventures, often straying from his wife, Hera. To help Zeus in his clandestine pursuits, Echo would distract Hera with her endless chatter whenever Hera came close to discovering Zeus's infidelities. Hera, frustrated by Echo's incessant talk and suspecting her of aiding Zeus, decided to punish the nymph.

In her wrath, Hera cursed Echo. From that moment on, Echo would no longer be able to speak freely. She could only repeat the last words spoken to her, doomed to forever echo the voices of others. This curse brought great sorrow to Echo, who longed to converse freely as she once had. Now, she wandered the forests, unable to communicate her thoughts and feelings, reduced to a mere reflection of others' words.

At the same time, there lived a youth of extraordinary beauty named Narcissus. Narcissus was the son of the river god Cephissus and the nymph Liriope. From his birth, it was clear that Narcissus was destined to be exceptionally handsome, a fact that did not go unnoticed by those around him. As he grew, so did his beauty, and soon he became the object of desire for both nymphs and mortals alike.

However, Narcissus was vain and proud. He reveled in the adoration of others but was indifferent to their feelings. He had no interest in love or companionship, and he spurned all those who tried to win his affection. Many suitors, both male and female, were left heartbroken by Narcissus's coldness, but none could move him to reciprocate their feelings.

One day, as Narcissus was wandering through the forest, Echo saw him and was instantly captivated by his beauty. Her heart swelled with love, and she longed to approach him, to speak to him, to tell him of her feelings. But she was bound by Hera's curse and could only repeat his words. Despite her limitations, Echo followed Narcissus through the woods, waiting for an opportunity to reveal herself.

Narcissus, unaware of Echo's presence, continued on his way until he became separated from his companions. Realizing he was alone, he called out, "Is anyone here?"

Echo, hiding among the trees, eagerly repeated, "Here!"

Startled, Narcissus looked around and called out again, "Come to me!"

Echo, thrilled to be able to speak, repeated his words, "Come to me!"

Hearing this, Narcissus grew curious, believing someone was nearby who wished to meet him. He continued to call out, and Echo continued to repeat his words. Eventually, Echo revealed herself and ran toward Narcissus, eager to embrace him.

However, when Narcissus saw her, he recoiled in disdain. "Away with you!" he shouted, pushing her aside. "I would rather die than let you have power over me."

Echo, heartbroken and humiliated, could only repeat his cruel words, "Let you have power over me... let you have power over me..." She fled deeper into the forest, hiding her face in shame, her love unfulfilled.

The rejection of Echo was just one of many cruelties Narcissus inflicted upon those who loved him. Eventually, the gods grew weary of his arrogance and decided to punish him for his heartlessness. Nemesis, the goddess of retribution, took it upon herself to teach Narcissus a lesson.

One day, as Narcissus was wandering through the woods, he came upon a clear, still pool of water. The surface of the water was like a mirror, perfectly reflecting everything around it. Thirsty from his journey, Narcissus knelt down to drink, but as he did so, he saw his reflection in the water.

Unaware that the image was his own, Narcissus was struck by the beauty of the face staring back at him. He fell deeply in love with the reflection, captivated by the eyes, the hair, the lips—everything about the figure in the water was perfect to him. He reached out to touch the face, but the water rippled, distorting the image and leaving him frustrated.

Narcissus became obsessed with the reflection, unable to tear himself away. He spoke to it, pleaded with it, but of course, it could not respond. He bent down to kiss it, only to have the water break apart under his touch. Day after day, Narcissus remained by the pool, refusing to eat or drink, consumed by his impossible love. He pined away, his body weakening as he wasted away, unable to leave the side of the one he loved.

As he lay dying, Narcissus finally realized that the face in the water was his own. "I loved myself in vain," he whispered as he drew his last breath. Echo, who had been silently watching from the shadows, repeated his words, "I loved myself in vain," as Narcissus's life slipped away.

After Narcissus's death, the gods took pity on him and transformed his body into a beautiful flower, which bore his name: the narcissus. The flower, with its delicate white petals and yellow center, grew by the edge of the pool where Narcissus had died, bending over the water as if still gazing at its own reflection.

Echo, consumed by grief, faded away until only her voice remained. She became nothing more than a sound, a disembodied echo that would repeat the words of others for eternity. Her love for Narcissus remained unfulfilled, her existence reduced to a haunting reminder of the tragic tale.

The story of Echo and Narcissus serves as a powerful lesson in Greek mythology, illustrating the dangers of vanity, unrequited love, and self-obsession. Narcissus's inability to love others and his eventual downfall highlight the consequences of excessive pride and self-admiration. Echo's fate, on the other hand, serves as a poignant reminder of the pain of unreturned affection and the sorrow that can result from it.

CHAPTER 17: APOLLO AND HYACINTHUS

In the ancient land of Sparta, a region known for its strength and valor, there lived a youth named Hyacinthus. Hyacinthus was the son of King Amyclas of Sparta and Queen Diomede, and from the moment of his birth, it was clear that he was no ordinary child. Blessed with extraordinary beauty, Hyacinthus was admired by all who beheld him. His striking features, golden hair, and bright, youthful charm made him the object of affection for mortals and gods alike.

Among the many who loved Hyacinthus, the most notable was Apollo, the god of the sun, music, poetry, and prophecy. Apollo, known for his own stunning beauty and grace, was captivated by the youth. The love that Apollo felt for Hyacinthus was deep and sincere, and it was returned in kind. The two became inseparable, spending their days together in the fields and woods, where they would engage in various pursuits, both playful and serious.

Apollo and Hyacinthus shared a bond that transcended the ordinary relationships between gods and mortals. Apollo, who was known for his many skills, took it upon himself to teach Hyacinthus various arts. Under Apollo's tutelage, Hyacinthus became a master of the lyre, an accomplished archer, and a skilled athlete. Apollo also introduced him to the mysteries of prophecy, sharing with him the secrets of the future.

The two would often engage in friendly competitions, testing their skills against each other in music, archery, and athletics. But it was in the sport of discus throwing that they found the greatest joy. The discus, a heavy, circular object made of bronze, was thrown for distance, and both Apollo and Hyacinthus excelled in this sport. Their competitions were always lighthearted, filled with laughter and camaraderie, as they reveled in each other's company.

Their bond was not merely one of teacher and student, nor simply of friends; it was a deep and abiding love that connected them. Apollo cherished every moment he spent with Hyacinthus, and the youth, in turn, adored the god who had become his closest companion and mentor. Their love was pure and joyous, and it seemed that nothing could ever separate them.

One day, as the sun shone brightly over the plains of Sparta, Apollo and Hyacinthus decided to spend the day outdoors, enjoying each other's company. The weather was perfect, with a gentle breeze rustling the leaves and the scent of wildflowers filling the air. They brought along a discus, intending to engage in their favorite pastime.

The two took turns throwing the discus, each trying to outdo the other with strength and precision. As usual, their competition was friendly and filled with laughter, with neither truly caring who won. When it was Apollo's turn, he took the discus and, using his divine strength, hurled it high into the sky. The discus soared through the air, glinting in the sunlight, and began its descent toward the earth.

Hyacinthus, eager to impress his beloved Apollo, ran after the discus, determined to catch it before it hit the ground. However, as the discus descended, something unexpected happened. Some versions of the myth suggest that the wind, perhaps guided by the jealousy of Zephyrus, the god of the west wind, altered the course of the discus. In other versions, it is simply a tragic accident. Whatever the cause, the discus struck Hyacinthus on the head with great force.

The impact was devastating. Hyacinthus collapsed to the ground, blood pouring from the wound on his head. Apollo, horrified, rushed to his side, cradling the boy's body in his arms. He tried desperately to stop the bleeding, using all his divine powers to heal the wound, but it was too late. The injury was fatal, and the life of Hyacinthus slipped away as Apollo held him, tears streaming down his face.

The death of Hyacinthus brought immense sorrow to Apollo, who was inconsolable in his grief. He had never known such pain, not even in his own immortal life. The guilt of having indirectly caused the death of his beloved weighed heavily on him. Apollo lamented the loss of Hyacinthus, crying out to the Fates, begging them to bring the youth back to life, but even the gods were powerless to reverse death.

Apollo refused to let Hyacinthus's memory fade into oblivion. He vowed that his love for the boy would be eternal, and he would ensure that Hyacinthus's name would be remembered forever. As a token of his love and in memory of the youth, Apollo decided to transform the blood that had spilled onto the ground into a beautiful flower. Where Hyacinthus's blood had soaked the earth, a delicate flower began to bloom. The petals of the flower were a deep purple, the color of mourning, and they bore markings that resembled the letters "AI," a symbol of Apollo's cries of grief.

This flower, which came to be known as the hyacinth, became a symbol of both the beauty and fragility of life, as well as a reminder of the deep love that had existed between Apollo and Hyacinthus. Apollo decreed that the hyacinth would forever be associated with his beloved, ensuring that Hyacinthus's name would be spoken for generations to come.

The hyacinth flower, which still blooms today, serves as a reminder of this ancient love story. It is said that every spring, when the hyacinths bloom, Apollo's love for Hyacinthus is renewed, and the god's sorrow is felt once more. The flower's beauty is a testament to the enduring nature of love, even in the face of loss and death.

In some versions of the myth, it is believed that Hyacinthus's spirit was taken to the Elysian Fields, the paradise reserved for the souls of heroes and the virtuous. There, he would live on, forever young and beautiful, free from the pain and suffering of the mortal world. Apollo, though heartbroken, could take solace in the knowledge that Hyacinthus had found peace.

CONCLUSION

As we reach the end of Greek Mythology: A Collection of Captivating Greek Myths, we reflect on the timeless stories that have not only entertained but also shaped our understanding of the world and ourselves. Greek mythology is more than a collection of ancient tales; it is a profound exploration of the human experience, filled with gods and goddesses who embody the full spectrum of human emotions, heroes who face extraordinary challenges, and monsters that symbolize our deepest fears.

Throughout this book, we have journeyed through the cosmos with the Olympian gods, witnessed the valor and tragedy of legendary heroes, encountered fearsome creatures that inhabit the edges of the known world, and delved into the rich cultural tapestry of ancient Greece. Each myth, with its unique characters and narratives, offers insight into the values, struggles, and aspirations of a civilization that has left an indelible mark on human history.

These myths have endured for thousands of years because they speak to universal truths about love, power, pride, and the consequences of our choices. They remind us of the complexities of life, the inevitability of fate, and the enduring quest for knowledge, justice, and redemption. Whether it is the cunning of Odysseus, the strength of Heracles, or the tragic fate of Oedipus, these stories continue to resonate with readers across generations, offering lessons that are as relevant today as they were in the distant past.

As you close this book, may the stories of Greek mythology continue to inspire you, spark your imagination, and deepen your appreciation for the rich cultural heritage that these myths represent. Whether you are drawn to the grandeur of the gods, the heroism of the mortals, or the mysteries of the mythical creatures, these tales offer a wealth of wisdom and wonder that transcends time. Greek mythology is a living tradition, one that continues to evolve and influence our world, reminding us of the power of storytelling and the enduring legacy of the ancient Greeks.

If you enjoyed this book, I kindly ask that you take a moment to leave a review on Amazon. Your feedback is invaluable and helps me tremendously in continuing to create books like this. Reviews not only provide encouragement but also help other readers discover the wonders of Greek mythology. Thank you for your support, and I hope these stories continue to bring you joy and inspiration.

Made in the USA
Columbia, SC
17 December 2024

49735413R00098